# Rural England

HARVINGTON, NEAR EVESHAM, WORCESTER.

# Rural England

## COTTAGE AND VILLAGE LIFE

### P.H. DITCHFIELD

Colour plates and line drawings by

### A.R. QUINTON

BRACKEN BOOKS
LONDON

# CONTENTS

# LIST OF ILLUSTRATIONS
## COLOURED PLATES

# LIST OF ILLUSTRATIONS

# LIST OF ILLUSTRATIONS

## LINE ILLUSTRATIONS

# PREFACE

THE love of country life is a plant of recent growth in the minds of dwellers in the city. On those who live amidst the fields and lanes of rural England it has always shed its fragrance, but we are so accustomed to its perfume that we rarely stop to consider whence this sweetness springs. In this book we have tried to understand why we admire the beauties of rural scenes, of the cots by the wayside, and in what their merit consists, and so to enable ourselves to appreciate more fully their charming character. The artist, Mr. Quinton, has depicted some of the most beautiful examples of rural homes that England affords. These I have tried to describe, to discover the secrets of their attractiveness, and to compare them with modern dwellings which lack their comeliness.

The study of English village life may be approached from various points of view. It presents a wide field for antiquarian research; and this I have previously attempted to explore in my book on "English Villages," published several years ago by Messrs. Methuen and Co. The story of domestic architecture as displayed in rural homes has been told by me in my books, published by Mr. Batsford, on "The Charm of the English Village" and "The Manor Houses of England." The genesis of the present work is the delightful series

# PREFACE

of sketches in colour which Mr. Quinton has depicted and are here reproduced. We have explored together some of the quaint nooks and corners, the highways and byways, of old England, and with pen and brush described them as they are at the present time. We have visited the peasant in his wayside cottage, watched the children at their games, the gossips on the bridge, the lace-maker plying her bobbins at her door, admired the flowers in her garden, entered the old village shop, and even " taken our ease at an inn." It is mainly the modern life of the hamlet that is here set forth, though the peel-towers of the Border Land, the homes of the statesmen and dalesmen, the church house and village green, have each a story to tell that may not be disregarded and blends itself with present-day conditions.

The eyes of our politicians are at the present time cast upon rural affairs, and town-bred speakers threaten us with many changes. Already they have wrought much mischief. The breaking-up of estates, caused by the heavy and merciless taxation levied on land, the dethronement of the squires and agricultural depression, have produced consternation in many village communities. Village industries that provided remunerative occupation for our rustics have been crushed out, and we may expect further losses and revolutions. Agitators are eager to pull down our old cottages and erect new ones which lack all the grace and charm of our old-fashioned dwellings. It is well to catch a glimpse of rural England before the transformation comes and to preserve a record of the beauties

# PREFACE

that for a time remain. This book is travelling to our country-
men across the seas, to America and Australia, and will recall
many happy memories of the Old Country, its rural scenes and
associations.

The author desires to express his gratitude to the artist,
Mr. Quinton, for the illustrations that adorn these pages, and
to the publisher, Mr. Dent, for many happy suggestions for the
production of this book.

P. H. DITCHFIELD

BARKHAM RECTORY
*October* 1912

The Church on the Hill, Kersey, Suffolk.

## IN THE COUNTRY

"SUMMER is a cumin in," sang the old monk of our Abbey of Reading as he heard the cuckoo chanting its merry notes and the kine lowing in the pasture and the deer calling in the-thickets; and though many centuries of springs have passed since the sunshine gladdened the heart of the black-robed Benedictine poet in the monastic cloister, we still welcome spring and the early summer days and chant their praises. The birds sing their love-ditties, the grass and wild-flowers and bursting leaves, the breezes blowing over the young grass of the fields, all proclaim with tender voice the joy of the year when " stern winter is past and the rain is over and gone ; the flowers appear on the earth and the time of the singing of birds is come. Arise, my love, my fair one, and come away."

The song comes fresh and clear to the ear wearied by the harsh sounds of the winter's roaring blasts, and fills with ecstasy the heart that has been numbed by the hard frost and the piercing icy storms. But even in winter the face of Nature, though wrinkled with cold, is not without its loveliness, just as the beauty of a fair woman with a brave heart fails not though her raven locks are turned to grey and time has chiselled lines that tell but of her perfections. The thousand dry twigs and branches of yonder oak covered with the rime of a sharp hoar-frost, each tiny grain glistening in the sunlight, look almost as beautiful as when they were clad in their summer foliage of green leaves. Hard and frozen was the ground and the streams were ice-bound. Snowstorms filled our lanes and covered the fields. Great drifts piled themselves high as miniature mountains. The farmer sat by his fire in the ingle-nook and scarcely a sound broke the stillness of the snow-bound village.

The country is ever changing, and sweet it is to watch the advancing season, to hear each fresh note, to mark the flowers awakening from their winter's sleep, until the time comes for them to sleep again and the crops are all gathered in, and the leaves are falling from the trees when touched by the frost and the mists and rains and chill winds betoken the decline of the year. And though the eye and ear delight in the passing pageant, though there are these constant scenes of change and the endless variety of Nature's ways, the country really never changes. Each spring the violets bloom, the lilies raise their heads in the garden, the swallows build their nests in the eaves, the rooks repair their old nests and breed their young. Each year the golden grain is gathered and the seed sown. It matters not whether you or I drop out of the picture. The roses would bloom just as brightly, the larks sing just as blithely, if we were not here to wonder at and admire the sweetness.

# LIFE OF RURAL ENGLAND

And so it is with the works of man, the ally of Nature. Along yonder road that runs so straight across the Downs the Roman legions marched. Alfred's Saxons chased the Danes down yonder hillside. Monks' hands reared yon grange and parish church, and built so surely and so well that their work has lasted through the centuries that have elapsed since they turned masons, and will last long after you and I are gathered to our fathers and rest beneath the shadow of the cross in God's hallowed acre. Cromwell's troopers galloped along that lane pursued by Rupert's cavaliers. There have been excitements at times when those troopers came back and turned the poor parson out of his rectory and a loud-voiced Puritan thundered forth from the pulpit about Mahershalah-hash-baz who made haste to divide the spoil. But soon quiet returns to the village again. Corn is sown and reaped. The sheep are climbing the hills as they do to-day, as they did when Alfred was chasing the Danes, as they will when we are gone to our rest. All is unchanged, this rural life of England.

And who is there who would love to have it changed ? There is no more beautiful thing on God's earth than an unspoilt English village. They are as varied as the faces of our friends and look at us with quite as friendly faces, and they are all beautiful unless they have been marred by modern innovations, by the production of strange anomalies and the association together of materials which Nature has not blended. Whether they be built of stone, or of timber, or brick that has been mellowed by the action of time and weather, or whether the houses composing them be tile-hung or weather-boarded, they are always pleasing to the eye, restful, and attractive.

Look at that beautiful little village of Carhampton, in the western shire of Somerset, its calm and peaceful village street with the tower of the church rising in the distance ; or see the old-world charm of the Kentish Groombridge, anciently belonging to the distinguished family of the Cobhams, who in 1285 had a royal licence to hold a weekly market. From this family it passed to the Wallers. Sir Richard Waller was a gallant soldier and fought at the battle of Agincourt, taking prisoner the Duke of Orleans, who lived at Groombridge twenty-four years. He liked his captivity so much that he rebuilt the old mansion, and was a benefactor to the neighbouring church of Speldhurst, over the porch of which his arms were placed. We English people are far too fond of pulling down our old buildings. Of course Speldhurst Church has been rebuilt. This was done in 1870, and I expect the Duke's arms disappeared then. However, no one has as yet destroyed the beauty of Groombridge. The village green remains, upon which two donkeys are grazing, and the old tile-hung cottages with attractive dormer windows jutting out of the roof are as attractive as ever, and the view of the walks is a dream of colour, with the mellowed brick and tile-hung houses, the tiled path and the flowers ablaze in their summer glory. In our survey of the hamlets and cottages of England we shall strive to learn the origin of things, how the village assumed its present shape, the causes that produced such divers arrangements of village-planning, the story of the development of the architectural features of the humbler sort of dwellings, the industries that flourished in their rural homes, the characters of the men that dwelt therein, their shrewdness, their faith, their superstitions, their customs. And as we admire the beauties of the English cottages we shall, perhaps, wonder at the men who could build for themselves such pleasing and enduring homes. These were not fashioned by skilled architects with carefully drawn plans, but by the peasants themselves, who wrought as best they could, sweetly, naturally, unaffectedly. They learnt the secrets of their art by their commune with Nature and from the traditions handed down from father to son from a remote past. The results of their handicraft we can see to-day, and learn much from the contemplation. From a study of the old we learn to construct what is new. It will, therefore, be our pleasure to journey together through many highways and byways of the Old Country, and note, with our artist's aid, what time has left of the ancient homes which our forefathers reared. We shall see the cottage of the Berkshire peasant and the Cornish fisher's hut, the lovely moorland shepherd's dwelling, the Sussex and East Anglian homesteads, and the nestling hamlets nigh the village church and manor-house. We shall wander through the cottage gardens and note the old-fashioned flowers that bloom therein, and feel the sentiment that sheds its glamour over all and endears to us the country life of England.

Nor is this study of the old-fashioned cottages of our country barren of results. They should be sketched, as our artist with skilled brush has so ably painted them, and preserved, not only because they are pretty subjects for artistic treatment, and not only because they are old. They are not merely keepsakes and curiosities. They are beautiful examples of the humbler kind of domestic architecture, and therefore of a peculiar value at a time when the humbler kind of domestic architecture is usually mean and debased beyond words. As the *Times* stated recently, " Good building will only flourish among us once again if we want it, and the taste for it is not likely to return unless it is quickened by the sight of the good building of the past. The more we destroy the more contented we shall remain with the worst faults in our present buildings, which are shamed by the virtues of the old." The study of the work of former ages should make men discontented with their present achievements and eager to build in the spirit that produced these quiet, unobtrusive beauties in the past.

Our artist has depicted for us many examples of delightful cottage architecture. Plain and humble they are, with no vain pretension, but they have a peculiar beauty of their own, and by their exquisite and simple naturalness attract the wonder of all who can admire what is beautiful and love what is good.

## II

## THE HAMLET UNDER THE HILL

In these days when we travel by rail or motor-car from town to town, from one end of England to the other, we hardly realise that each little village through which we pass has a separate entity, a sturdy independence, a social life apart from its fellows. It has peculiarities of its own, likes and dislikes, a certain pride and ambition, and usually looks down with scorn upon its nearest neighbour. Two villages standing near each other are often great rivals. Not long ago the champion fighter of one village would, with his mates, march off to the rival village, and throw down his cap on the village green. At this signal the champion of the other, who happened to be the blacksmith, would be dragged away from his smithy by his friends and willy-nilly be bound to fight a battle royal with his challenger, who in this primitive fashion was asserting the independence of his native hamlet.

In these days we hear much of town-planning, of the arrangement of so-called model villages. Who was the author of the plans of our old villages? These were devised in very early times by force of circumstance, by necessity, without any rules of art or æsthetic regulations. Some arose around the gates of a monastic house like Battle or Glastonbury. A monastery needed masons and carpenters and ploughmen and a small army of workmen to build and keep in repair the buildings, to farm the monastic lands. Hence there arose around it a town or village, with an inn or guest-house for pilgrims; and the cottages cluster around the monastery like children holding the gown of their good mother.

Then there are castle-villages that owe their origin to the presence of some lordly castle, such as Kenilworth, which arose around the Norman keep of Geoffroi de Clinton and the princely palace of the Earl of Leicester. Castles needed masons and artificers. They afforded, too, protection in troublous times, and under the shadow of the castle houses grew and felt themselves safe from roving bands of robbers or the armed hosts of lawless barons.

Castle Elmley, in Worcestershire, takes its name from the fortress which Robert Dispensator reared soon after the Norman Conquest. It passed to the Beauchamps, Lords of Warwick, who in the thirteenth century made their Warwickshire castle their home, and Elmley Castle became a deserted ruin. Perhaps the little village was happier without its castle, and at the present time looks very calm and peaceful with its half-timbered and brick houses erected on their stone foundations and its trees in its main street growing beside a running watercourse.

Dunster, in Somerset, is a castle village or market town dominated by the ancient castle of the Mohuns which held out for the Empress Maud in the disastrous civil war of King Stephen's reign

CARHAMPTON, SOMERSET.

THE WALKS, GROOMBRIDGE, KENT.

Geoffrey Luttrell, who held it in the time of King John, took a foremost part in helping the warlike Archdeacon of Taunton, William de Wrotham, to rule the king's navy. Dunster Castle was the last fortress in Somerset to capitulate to the Parliamentarian forces commanded by the redoubtable Robert Blake. George Luttrell, Sheriff of Somerset, a descendant of the aforenamed Geoffrey, about the year 1600 erected that picturesque market cross, or yarn market, as it is sometimes called, which appears in the illustration. It is octagonal in shape, with curious gables jutting out from each face of the long, sloping roof. It is crowned with a vane bearing the initials G. L., which are those of the grandson of the builder. The arrangement of the timbers extending radially from the centre of the cross is somewhat remarkable. One of them has been pierced by a cannon-ball shot from the castle during the siege in the Civil War. This cross was used as a yarn market, Dunster at one time being famous for its " Kersey " cloths and " Dunsters." It is pleasant to know that the castle is still, after the lapse of seven centuries, the residence of the Luttrell family, the present owner being Captain Alexander Fownes Luttrell, a descendant of the Geoffrey Luttrell who held the castle in the time of King John. Dunster is a quaint, old-fashioned, typical Somerset village, and fair to look upon, as the brush of our artist discloses. It is rich, too, in the memorials of the piety of its people. It has several crosses and a notable church, the choir of which was the minster of the monks

# THE COTTAGES AND VILLAGE

of Dunster Priory, while the nave was the parish church. Hence at the Dissolution of Monasteries it was spared, and not even the choir pulled down as at Malmesbury, Waltham, and elsewhere.

In very many cases the modern village is directly descended from its old Roman sire, or even pre-Roman ancestor. It is not uncommon to find the church and manor-house lying near together, and close beside them the remains of a Roman villa, and not far away a Roman cemetery. Roman foundations and coins prove in many cases the continuity of the village community. The Saxon invaders found many of the villages in existence when they came. As colonists they would not be so foolish as to make fresh clearings in the forests and found new settlements when they had lands already farmed and tilled; and however much they avoided the walled t ns of Roman Britain, they certainly had no such antipathy to the occupation of its villas and rural villages.

Most modern villages have a "street"—not what a townsman knows by that name, a fine thoroughfare with grand shops and houses on each side, but a simple village road connecting the cottages with the church and manor-house. We have a "street" in my little village of Barkham leading from the manor to the church, with a farm on one side and a dozen scattered cottages on the other. The name is Roman. It is the old *strata via*, or paved way, and connects the modern village with its old-time progenitor. The planning of the village accords with the old lines.

I have often sketched the plan of an ideal village in my books, and that which I set forth in my earliest book on the subject, entitled " English Villages," * perhaps explains best its component parts. It is an ideal village, not an actual photograph, a composite sketch that reproduces most of the elements of which an ordinary village is composed. There is the church and manor-house side by side and the old rectory. The church was " the centre of the old village life, religious, secular and social."† The manor-house was the residence of the lord of the manor or his bailiff, and the land around it was in demesne, *i.e.,* it belonged to the lord for his own use,‡ and so distinguished from the land occupied by his tenants, who were obliged to do some services for their lord, such as ploughing or harvesting on the demesne land. A manor was land "granted by the king to some baron or gentleman as an inheritance for him and his heirs, with the exercise of such jurisdiction as the king saw fit to grant, and subject to the performance of such services and yearly rents as were by the grant required."§ Some manor-lords had to provide one or more armed men to go with the king when he warred in Wales, or to present a rose when the king should pass near the house. Very many and some very ridiculous services were required. One poor lord had to hold the head of the king when he crossed the

* Methuen and Co.    † "English Villages" (Methuen and Co.).

‡ *Demesne* is an old French word meaning the same as the Latin *dominium,* right of ownership, and is derived from *dominus,* which signifies lord or master and is connected with *domus,* or house.

§ "Guide to the Public Records," by Mr. Scargill-Bird.

seas. A survival of these customs of what are called *petit sergeanty* is that requiring the successive Dukes of Marlborough to present to the king on the anniversary of the battle of Blenheim a little flag, by which custom they hold the manor and palace of Blenheim. And as the lord owed his duty to the king, so those who held land under him were required to render to him divers services. He had the power of holding in his manor a domestic court called a court baron, in which alienations and disputes as to property were arranged, by-laws made, and breaches of such presented to a jury and visited with a fine. He also held a court leet, which tried small criminal offences.

In spite of the changes wrought by time, the lord of the manor has still some rights and privileges; he may, and still does in some cases, hold his courts, and is a person who cannot be quite disregarded. The mill was an important building; it usually belonged to the lord, and the tenants were obliged to bring their corn to be ground there. It is usually on the banks of the stream that runs through the village. Our forefathers were wise enough to know the need of the existence of water, and usually planted their settlements along the course of some stream. The street or road by the side of which the principal cottages and farms were erected often runs parallel with this stream, which was the only means of draining. In many cases the houses are grouped round a village green, which was the place of amusement for the people. Here fairs were held and the may-pole raised, and the villagers had the right to turn out cattle and geese, and there is a pond in the centre where ducks disport themselves.

The village and the manor were not identical. Sometimes there are two, three, or more manors in a village, and its plan often retains evidences of this old division. Thus at Fritwell, in Oxfordshire, there are two sections of the village separated by a common. These correspond to the two original manors, and a third group of houses indicates a reputed manor formed later by a Duke of Ormond.

There are various houses in the village which invite inspection. There is the old inn with its swinging signboard. The entrance to the inn-yard is very narrow, under an archway, and requires some skill in driving to steer your horse and dog-cart through without grazing the sides. The yard presents a fine view of quaint gables, tiled roofs, and old-fashioned stables. Part of a gallery runs round the yard, where the guests used to stand and watch the mountebanks and strolling players in olden days. The chief room is paved with red bricks, and it contains some nice old furniture and some pewter plates and mugs and wax flowers under glass cases, and copper saucepans, and some hunting pictures.

There is a quaint old building near the church which we shall visit presently. It is called the church house, and belonged to the churchwardens, who let it to wandering merchants for the storing of their goods, and was often the scene of rural revelry when " church ales " were held for the good of the poor or the support of some necessary repairs of the church, or other worthy object.

A long, low building bordering on the green, with some patient old folk sitting in the vine-clad porches or tending their flowers, is the almshouse of the village, erected by an ancestor of the present squire in Tudor times. He had gained much wealth out of the spoils of the monasteries, and thought he ought to spend some of his increased riches on the infirm old folk of his village. He built also a grammar school for the young people, but it has seen better days, and is only an elementary school now, and can scarcely succeed in satisfying those trying gentlemen from London who come down to our villages and worry the poor parson's life out of him by their requirements as to increased school accommodation, furniture, drainage, and repairs.

And then there are the buildings, the cottages and farmhouses, the church, which shows evidences of the care of the people in its fabric, containing specimens of the work of all Gothic styles from Norman times onwards, the manor-house, a perfect example of fine Tudor building, than which nothing can be more beautiful, more homely, more satisfying.

Such treasures does the first glance at our village reveal. But that is not all. It is set in a framework of dark elms, of oaks that are as old almost as the surrounding hills, and could tell stories of many generations of squires and farmers who have lived and died while they have been growing and maturing. The fruit-

EVENING, ELMLEY CASTLE, WORCESTER

ELMLEY CASTLE stands on the Bredon Hills, and tells of the earliest
settlement of the ancient, widespread, but now extinct family of
Beauchamp. In the female line it survives, and its blood is mingled
with that of our Royal Family and not a few of our ancient nobility
and county families. " It is toward evening, and the day is far
spent," and the labourer is performing his last daily task of carrying
home the water from the well. The sketch shows a pleasing row
of cottages. The wattle and daub of the lower panels of the wall
had become worn and rotten by the weather, and had to be replaced
by courses of red brick. An oriel window of pleasing design, supported on a moulded base, juts out from the surface of the wall.
Notice the noble chimney and the lattice windows, and the gracefully
curved thatch—a very pretty picture.

OLD COTTAGE, BIGNOR, SUSSEX

BIGNOR is a quiet agricultural village, and not the least interesting
of its specimens of domestic architecture is this charming old cottage.
It is built in three bays, the central one receding, the roof over it
being supported by curved braces. The oblong openings between
the upright and horizontal timbers have been filled with bricks
when the old wattle and daub decayed, and these are arranged in
herring-bone fashion. The two external bays have an over-sailing
upper storey supported upon imposts. The foundations of the
house are built of local stone, and the doors are set above this where
the timber-work begins, and are reached by a graceful flight of
steps protected by a hand-rail. The windows are of lattice-work,
and the roof of thatch wrought with spars to keep it in its place.

trees in the orchards are in full bloom, as in the delightful village of Dossington, near Shakespeare's home at Stratford-on-Avon ; and the flowers in the cottage gardens are bright with colour, while the green verdure of the bright common forms a cheerful foreground to the picture. Such is the setting of the gems which we are examining, and now we will inspect the jewels in detail.

## III

## THE COT BY THE WAYSIDE

THE appreciation of cottage-building is a plant of recent growth, a newly found truth, and, therefore, precious. The cottage has a beauty that is all its own, a directness, a simplicity, a variety and an inevitable quality. The intimate way in which cottages ally themselves with the soil and blend with the ever-varied and exquisite landscape, the delicate harmonies that grow from their gentle relationship with their surroundings, the modulation from man's handiwork to God's enveloping world that binds one to the other without discord or dissonance—all this is a revelation to eyes unaccustomed to seek out the secrets of art and nature. " It is only a cottage," people say, without realising the importance which it really occupies in the story of English building, apart from the fact that they are very picturesque and very beautiful. They are that—at least we think so now, when we are delivered from the old *régime* of artificiality and false standards passed away in the last century, and new ideals, which were really a revival of the old, taught us sounder principles of taste. It would be hard to exaggerate the value of these little English cottages from this aspect of beauty alone. No one can deny that

16

the period of the decline and fall of English architecture had reached its lowest depth in the early nineteenth century. It could sink no lower, and then there dawned upon eyes that had somehow recovered their sight and could appreciate what they saw a glimpse of a typical English cottage. It was like finding amidst dust and cobwebs a precious mediæval manuscript bright with the illuminations of the old monks ; or a grand fourteenth-century walled-up window amid the vanities of Strawberry Hill Gothic. Cottage-building is neither Gothic nor Classic ; it is just good, sound, genuine and instructive English work, and when we can appreciate that we can learn to build the lofty minster or the mansion in a style of which no one need be ashamed. One other note we must make before we turn over the pages of our pictures and admire their beauties ; and that is this. The great era of architectural triumphs came to an end in the fifteenth century. The building of minsters and parish churches ceased entirely ; the erection of mansions and manor-houses proceeded at first with conspicuous success in the reigns of Elizabeth and James I., but the art rapidly declined and sank swiftly in the dark days of the later eighteenth century. But all the time the poor and middle classes were building, quietly and simply, untroubled by any controversies concerning the relative advantages of Renaissance or Gothic styles. They built for use, and carried on the traditions of their fathers and forefathers, frankly, simply, and directly ; and it is this that makes their buildings valuable to us. They have preserved for us the laws and traditions and records of a time that has passed away; and if we would regain what we have lost we must study the relics that time has spared us, and without slavishly imitating, as Horace Walpole copied his ruined abbeys, build in the spirit which produced such excellent work.

But what is a cottage? If we search the dry and musty tomes of English law books we find that, according to a statute of 4 Edward I., a cottage is a house with any land attached to it. It can date its pedigree back earlier than that. The *cottarii* or *bordarii* of the Domesday Survey were cottagers, those who dwelt in cots or cottages, were freemen, but were obliged to do some fixed services for the lord of the manor, and could not leave his estate to work elsewhere. When in the fifteenth and early sixteenth centuries the English wool trade was most prosperous, and land-lords turned their agricultural land into sheep-runs, fewer labourers were required and there was a great destruction of cottages. In the reign of Henry VII., in A.D. 1489, it was found necessary to pass an Act of Parliament prohibiting the wholesale pulling down of farms and cottages. Moreover, labourers used to sleep in their employer's house and have their meals in the hall with the family, though at a separate table. But in the time of Queen Elizabeth cottages were again required, and were then re-erected. An Act* of her reign tells of the building of many such dwellings, as its object was " for avoiding of the great inconveniences which are

* 31 Elizabeth c. 7.

found by experience to grow by the erectinge and buyldinge of great nombers and multitude of cottages which are dayly more and more increased in mayni parts of this realm." It orders that no one is to build or convert dwellings into cottages without setting apart at least four acres of ground to each. It excepts from the rule towns, mines, factories, and cottages for seafaring folk, under-keepers, and the like. In this provision the order anticipates the modern dream of beneficent legislation of "three acres and a cow." We gather from this that in the days of Queen Elizabeth cottage-building was vastly increased, and that old farmhouses and other buildings, as they fell into disuse owing to the erection of newer and more commodious houses, were converted into cottages for the accommodation of the increased number of agricultural labourers.

Then arose some of those beautiful rural homes which are still with us, and many examples are set forth in these pages. Some have the curse of poverty stamped upon them, and I would distinguish a cottage from a hovel—a small space enclosed by four mud walls and covered with sheltering thatch—as well as from one of those absurd lodges with Corinthian pillars and pseudo-Gothic windows erected on some estates in a period of debased taste. The English cottage rejects the poverty of the hovel, as well as the frippery decorations of "the grand style."

"Houses are built to live in and not to look upon," sagely remarks Lord Bacon; "therefore let Use be preferred before

# THE COTTAGES AND VILLAGE

Uniformity, except where both may be had." The builders of the sixteenth century were not unaware of this principle, and acted on it, though in seeking utility they achieved wonders in the way of beauty.

Before we examine the various styles and materials used in the construction of our cottage homes, which depend upon the

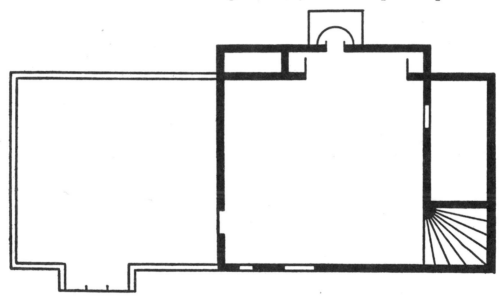

geological features of the districts where they were built, it may be well to discover their plan. This is very similar in all parts of the country. The simplest plan is an oblong with two storeys, subsequent additions having usually been made. The above plan is not an uncommon one.* The part enclosed in unblacked lines is an early addition. You will observe the central chamber with large wide fireplace and ingle-nook, the larder, and staircase in one corner with stairs formed round a newel. After the date

* "Old Cottage and Domestic Architecture in South-west Surrey," by Ralph Nevill, F.S.A., F.R.I.B.A.

DOSSINGTON, NEAR STRATFORD-ON-AVON

In the county of Gloucester, seven miles from Evesham and six from Chipping Campden, in the heart of the Cotswolds, lies Dossington. The apple-trees are in bloom, and the spring flowers are awakening from their winter sleep. This seventeenth-century cottage has weathered many winters, and the passage of time has but added to its beauty. It preserves the tradition of the central hall with a projecting wing attached to it, its plan being in the shape of the letter L. It is a simple timber-framed house, with the upper storey slightly projecting, and a tiled roof. As in many old houses, its timbers have become warped in places, and have assumed a graceful curve over the doorway.

DUNSTER, SOMERSET.

1600, straight stairs came into fashion, and were often formed by cutting steps in a solid balk of oak. You will notice the oven at the back of the fireplace. This is often of later date, as cottagers probably in olden days baked their bread in the baking-ovens attached to their employers' houses. Moreover, village bakers plied their trade as they do now. But in the sixteenth century and later the cottagers found it more economical to make these useful additions to rural abodes. They are sometimes quite large, and I knew a man who used to make an old oven his bed-chamber, though happily for him the fire was not lighted. In many cottages the large fireplace and ingle-nook have been bricked up. The modern labourer's wife wants a kitchen range and likes not the primitive style of cookery. Hence the old ingle-nooks have vanished and the fireplace fitted with less snug but more convenient modern culinary appliances. Gone, too, are the iron fire-dogs which gave a draught to the wood fire, and carried two loose square iron bars for the support of the cooking-pot. Sometimes there was a branched top to the iron dog for holding a cup of hot spiced ale, which was grateful and comforting on a cold winter's evening. The old methods of cooking were not to be despised. Joints were roasted on spits, either a large basket one for holding a joint of beef, or one with prongs, and to these was attached a wheel which was turned by a smoke-jack in the chimney.

But we must build our cottage before we examine the details of its domestic economy. The charming cottage at Bignor, in Sussex, a county of delightful homesteads, is built in three bays, the central one receding, the roof of which is supported by curved braces. It is a half-timbered house, like most of those depicted by our artist, who has a penchant for that method of construction. The oblong openings between the perpendicular and horizontal timbers are filled in with wattle and daub, and, where this has become decayed, with bricks, and these are arranged in herring-bone fashion, which method of building has come down to us from Saxon times, stone herring-bone work being usually deemed a peculiarity of Anglo-Saxon construction. But it must be noticed that this, and many similar houses, were built in bays, " the simplest form of construction being the house of one bay. Two pairs of bent trees (whence the term ' roof-tree ' seems to have been derived) were set up about sixteen feet apart. The gable end of many an old Cheshire cottage shows the persistence of this traditional type." * In Yorkshire and in other parts of England it is not uncommon to find the stables, barn, and dwelling-house all under the same roof and in one line. Hence each part of the structure corresponded in length to that which was required for the plough-team of two pairs of oxen.† A survey of the estates of the Earl of Arundel records "a dwelling house of four bayes a stable being an outshut and other outhouses are seven bayes besides a barne of four bayes."

* "Half-timbered Architecture of Cheshire," by C. H. Minshull ("Memorials of Old Cheshire ").

† We have no space to explain the whole subject of bays. The reader is referred to " The Evolution of the English House," by S. O. Addy (Social English Series).

Shakespeare may be quoted as a witness of this when he makes Pompey say in " Measure for Measure," " If this law hold in Vienna ten year, I'll rent the fairest house in it after threepence a bay."

That Bignor cottage, formerly the dwelling of a yeoman, and now a village shop, which we have so much admired, and serves to illustrate this story of the bays, reminds us of other interesting things that the village contains. These are—not the bays—the wondrous yews in the churchyard. We have been told that yews were grown in churchyards for the furnishing of bows for our English archers, who struck terror into the hearts of the French and won fame on many a foreign battlefield. But we think that the yew-tree is there for a sacred and symbolical reason, signifying the Resurrection. However that may be, there they grow venerable yet flourishing nigh Bignor Church; and not only does the village contain the remains of one of the most perfect Roman villas in England, with beautiful mosaic pavements, but—more nearly connected with our present subject—in the above-mentioned cottage, the quaintest and most curious little rural shop in the county. It is nigh the church, and there it stands with its diamond-paned windows, oak timbers, crazy doorway and approach by a flight of steep steps, a venerable relic of antiquity which we trust Bignor will long preserve.

But *revenons à nos moutons*, or rather to cottage architecture. The earliest cottages were built in the shape of an inverted boat. Two pairs of forks were set out at distances of a bay apart, and then beams or boards stretched across, and covered with thatch, the covering extending to the ground. Walls were an afterthought. We are so accustomed to having walls to our houses, and the roof resting on them, that we can hardly understand this primitive style of dwelling, which resembled a boat turned upside down. There are only two houses of this kind that remain, as far as we are aware ; one at Scrivelsby, in Lincolnshire, vulgarly known as " Tea-pot Hall," and the other at Didcot, in Berkshire. Such cottages resemble booths or tents, and were evidently based upon that model. There is a so-called oratory of Gallerius near Dingle, in the West of Ireland, built of stone, of similar shape. A remembrance of this boat-like shaped building is preserved in our word " nave," as of a church, which is the Latin *navis*, a ship.

We have so much to tell of Rural England that it is impossible for us here to trace the gradual development of our cottage architecture, and to show how the forked-shaped buildings took to themselves walls, still preserving the forked basis of construction. We have seen how a new era of cottage-building started in Elizabeth's time ; and it will be sufficient for our present purpose if we take that reign as a starting-point for a beginning of the story of the humbler form of domestic architecture. We see the cottages to-day that often date their foundation from that period. We admire their beauties. Perhaps it may be well to understand why we admire them, in what their merit consists ; and so enable ourselves to appreciate more fully their charming character.

The commonest form of cottage of the better sort erected during the sixteenth and seventeenth centuries is that framed after the model of the manor-house. Every one is familiar with the story of the development of the English manor-house, a story that I have already told and need not here repeat.* The cottages followed the same plan, as several of our illustrations show. There is an **L**-shaped cottage at Carhampton, to which we have already referred. Cowdray's Cottage (p. 51) is based upon the same plan. In the village street of Kersey (p. 24) there is an **H**-shaped house, and the view of East Hagbourne (p. 177) shows another example of the **L**-shaped cottage. At Steventon there is an **E**-planned house. Possibly some of the cottage homes here depicted have seen better days, and were originally substantial farmhouses, now converted into cottages. They do not always make the best rural homes. The neighbours are too near together. Sometimes they quarrel and " do not speak "; and relations become strained when there is a common pump, and both housewives want to draw water at the same time, and children will trespass sometimes, and look over a neighbour's fence, if not pick flowers just on the other side. Peace does not always reign when tempers are ruffled, and though proximity often brings love, it sometimes fosters dislike, and affairs do not run smoothly. It is, however, interesting to notice the continuance of tradition in the planning and evolving of cottage architecture.

* *Cf.* " Manor-Houses of England," by P. H. Ditchfield (Batsford, London).

# COTTAGES OF RURAL ENGLAND

Another plan of cottage-building is the squatter's cottage, a very simple and homely structure. You will have noticed in many villages along the side of the road with gardens touching the hedge of the fields little cottages built on land that has been an encroachment. There are several houses of this description in my parish of Barkham. Country roads were wide; they were repaired and gravelled. The ruts were deep and the way almost impassable, just like the green lanes in this village, along which if you ride your horse's hoofs stick so fast that you are afraid lest he will leave one behind him. So the carters drove whither they listed along this wide track. Gipsies pitched their tents on this disused land. No one thought it of any value, and then the squatter came and reared his simple dwelling of two rooms and covered it with thatch. He chose the materials that came readiest to his hand, bricks or cob, stone or timber, which his employer carted for him. Most of the work he did himself with the help of a kindly neighbour; and then he would raise a bank and enclose a small garden, and plant a hedge of elders because they grow quickly. And thus he became a miniature landowner, paying no rent, perhaps a small due to the lord of the manor for a few years, but was practically his own landlord and ruler of his own little domain. He becomes very proud of his cottage, and proud of himself, and develops into a sturdy and independent person, one of the best of labourers, happy and contented.

## IV

## HOW COTTAGES WERE BUILT: A RAMBLE THROUGH THE SHIRES

FEW people in these days enjoy the pleasures of a walking tour in England. It was the best method of seeing the country, of learning rustic ways, manners, and opinions. You could chat with the lonely shepherd on the hills, the labourer returning from his work, and pick up many treasures of wayside wisdom. For this primitive method of locomotion we have substituted the bicycle and the motor-car. These present some advantages. We can extend our gaze, and take a rapid survey of the country, and although our impressions are less enduring and our glimpses of rural life more fleeting, we can journey further afield, to north and south, to east and west, and compare one shire with another. Each shire has its own characteristics, its customs, laws, dialect, and modes of industry, as I have tried to show in my book on the counties of England.* And as we roam among the villages of England we notice their diversity and the variety of materials of which the buildings are constructed. As a recent writer says: " Ever present there is a feeling of harmony. The harmony that should exist between a building and its surroundings is probably nowhere better illustrated

* " The Counties of England " (2 vols.; Messrs. G. Allen and Co.).

# THE COTTAGES AND VILLAGE

than in the cottage. Set amid natural scenes in rich valleys or clustering on the hill-sides, they seem part of the landscape ; no conflicting note meets the eye, and building blends with building and their environment."

Some of the best examples of stone-built houses are found in the village of Broadway, in Worcestershire. Gothic traditions of

THE GREEN, BROADWAY, WORCESTERSHIRE

workmanship linger on to the present day in the Cotswold region, and masons continue to build as their fathers did before them, and we find in that district a perfect survival of the Middle Ages. We give a sketch of the village green at the foot of the hilly main street, surrounded with fine old houses and cottages with mullioned windows and wood mouldings, moulded doorways, and many other Gothic features. Amongst these Broadway houses we find such gems of domestic architecture as the Abbot's Grange, wherein the Abbots of Pershore used to retire for rest and refreshment, a long grey building of dressed stone and rubble, the centre broken by two gables. In spite of its six centuries of existence it is a wonderfully complete example of the mediæval home of a manorial lord. The Lygon Arms Inn is an early seventeenth-

THE PLAGUE COTTAGES, EYAM, DERBYSHIRE

century building, picturesque and imposing, and the humbler dwellings all show the evidences of Gothic tradition and good masonry.

North-Country cottages and farmsteads have their own peculiarities. We will first travel to Eyam, in the beautiful region of Derbyshire, styled the Queen of the Peak, and that a widowed one. She stands alone among the hills, the solemn monument of a mighty woe, the dreadful plague, the records of which stir the

# THE COTTAGES AND VILLAGE

heart though more than two centuries have rolled away since the arrival of that dread visitant. Eyam stands on the great belt of oolite limestone, and her cottages of grey stone harmonise well with the rocky heights of the surrounding hills. They are generallym antled with ivy, adorned with fruit-trees, and shaded by wide-spreading sycamores. The grey tower of the church rises above the cottages from the centre of a circle of beautiful linden trees guarding the precincts of the dead. The cottage shown in the illustration is the identical cottage in which the plague began its destructive course. It stands at the east end of the Hall garden, and the plague was conveyed thither by a box containing some tailor's patterns in cloth and some old clothes sent from London to a tailor who lodged in this house, then inhabited by the Cooper family, in the year 1666. We need not tell again the story of the Eyam plague, which carried off 259 victims (five-sixths of the total population); of the self-sacrifice and courage of the inhabitants, who confined themselves to the village lest they should carry the infection elsewhere, and the heroism of the rector, the Reverend William Mompesson, who refused to leave his flock; and of his no less heroic wife, who died of the plague. Some of the walls of the cottage have been renewed since that dread period of Eyam's history, but the interior is the same as when the fatal box arrived containing the germs of the contagious malady.

From Derbyshire to Yorkshire is only a step, and though many

The Village Street, Kersey, Suffolk.

FARMHOUSE, WELFORD-ON-AVON, GLOUCESTER

WELFORD-ON-AVON, Shakespeare's Avon, boasts of many good cottages with thatched roofs and dormer windows. It has a fine church and a grand old lych-gate, and there a may-pole stands, the successor of a very ancient one, around which the villagers danced in the days of Queen Bess. Looking down upon the one-storeyed cottages stands a good farmhouse, shown in the illustration, of half-timbered construction, tiled roof, and graceful gables ; and dignity is given to the house by the noble brick chimney, consisting of twin shafts, octagonal in plan, crowned by a neatly formed head. It is spring-time, and a glorious wealth of blossom adorns the fruit-trees and gives a promise of a bountiful fruit harvest.

a beautiful dale of the broad-acred shire has been doomed to the relentless spread of huge factories, belching forth black smoke, and of hideous streets of workmen's cottages, there are many cottages in the moors that have their own peculiar characteristics. Many old moorland houses were constructed with forks without side-walls, like an overturned boat, similar to those I have already described, and the side-walls were not added until 1656. Some dalesmen's houses have the dwelling-house, barn, and stables or cowhouse all under one roof. In the centre is the barn or threshing-floor, with a large pair of folding doors at one end and a small winnowing door at the other. On one side is the dwelling-house, and on the other the stables or ox-house. Sometimes the central part was a sort of passage with doors leading on one side to the habitation of the family, and the other to that of the animals, together with a barn. The reason why we call the entrance to a house the threshold is because the threshing-floor was placed there. In the dalesman's house he used to feed not only his family, but his labourers, who arranged themselves according to seniority at a long table remote from the fire, while he and his family sat at a round table near the hearth. There is a continuance of Scandinavian tradition in these combined houses, as their plan and arrangement correspond very closely with those of the old Norse house.* When Canon Atkinson called at Danby on his not very reverend predecessor, he visited a house very

* *Cf.* " Evolution of the English House," by S. O. Addy, p. 62.

similar to that which has just been described.\*    The cottage at Routh is a simple example of a Yorkshireman's plain dwelling.

When there is an absence of stone and the far-reaching forests extended their sway, in the western counties, in Berkshire, Surrey,

COTTAGE AT ROUTH, YORKSHIRE

Sussex, Kent, and elsewhere, houses built of timber are the most usual.    In Cheshire, Shropshire, and Herefordshire there is that beautiful, soft, warm sandstone of which Chester Cathedral and many a less important edifice are constructed; and as timber was plentiful there also we find those picturesque "magpies," or black and white dwellings, made of timber and plaster, that take their name from the bird of omen.    They contribute greatly

* *Cf.* "Forty Years in a Moorland Parish," by Canon Atkinson, p. 43.

to the picturesqueness of the Palatinate. One of the shire's architectural experts tells us:

"Here it may be a cluster of quaint cottages, or perhaps a single cottage of comely proportions nestling in some sequestered spot, or one of those moated granges or sturdy farmsteads that dot the countryside; or there it may be a more elaborate and ornate example, some 'stately home' attesting the skilful handiwork of the *faber lignarius* who centuries ago followed his calling with such excellent and enduring results, his fitly and soundly framing of the building together having enabled it to withstand the action of time and weather—if so by good fortune it managed to escape that more fatal enemy fire, whose ravages are no doubt responsible for the disappearance of many an architectural treasure, which, had a more resistant material been employed, might have survived to shed additional lustre on the country, already so renowned for its half-timbered treasures."

Just as I am writing the news comes that Carden Hall, one of Cheshire's famous "magpies," has been doomed to destruction by a disastrous fire. Another cause for their dilapidation has been that Cheshire was a great theatre of fighting in the great Civil War, and the good gentlemen of the country fortified and garrisoned their houses for the king. There is scarcely one that was not besieged and attacked, and doubtless many a picturesque farmhouse and cottage shared their fate. Possibly the Cheshire houses were not always "black and white," but that the timbers were tarred for the purpose of preservation in later times. Happily this mode of building is still preserved in the county, as the Duke of Westminster and other landlords continue to construct farms and cottages on their estates in the old " Cheshire style." And then we have parts of England where clay is plentiful, as in East Anglia ; and there the art of brick-making flourished, conveyed there by immigrant and industrious Flemings, and there we find some of the triumphs of brickwork, though they are not confined to that region, and plenty of good work in that material is found in conjunction with timber-framed houses. In districts destitute of stone cob-walled cottages are plentiful. Cob is mud, and layers of mud and straw were built up slowly but surely, the builder only adding about an inch a day, waiting for each layer to dry before he proceeded with the rest. You will see such cottages in Devonshire, whitewashed and roofed with thatch, brown and soft as the fur of a mole. The grandsire of my gardener in Suffolk built for himself a house, using clay from a dry pond in a similar fashion, and it has weathered the storms of East Anglia for at least two generations.

In Cambridgeshire, too, we find cottages built of sun-dried mud or clay for the walls, and also in the New Forest. Mr. Charles E. Clayton states that many of these mud-built cottages still remain. " The walls of them are formed of clay mixed with chopped straw and stones, packed down between boards or hurdles, these latter being removed when the clay dried and hardened.

THE BROOK, STEVENTON, BERKS

FEW villages possess such delightful bits of half-timbered domestic architecture as Steventon, dating back to the fifteenth, sixteenth, and seventeenth centuries. This corner with the brook and the old cottage makes a charming picture. In the coaching age it was an important little place on the Oxford and Southampton road. Here are still to be found primitive porches, old roofs and gables, lattice windows and ancient doorways, testifying to the abundance of oak and to the skill of the local carpenters. The interiors are panelled with oak, and have massive tie-beams, curious staircases, and one of the houses, dated 1637, has a pargetted front with barge-boards and two curiously panelled and painted rooms. Above the fireplace in one room are two panels on which landscapes have been painted, and the kitchen has three similar works of art.

CHIDDINGSTONE, KENT.

The surface is sometimes whitewashed, but often left uncoloured, and the walls, which are often two feet thick, appear very durable, some of the cottages being of two storeys, with stairways and other joinery ingeniously fixed to the mud walls by wood pegs with

A FELL-SIDE FARM, CUMBERLAND

wedged ends. In one case the writer found a recent brick casing over the original mud wall." *

Granite is the usual building-stone in Cornwall. It is a land of colour, this rugged, beautiful Cornwall, where the tossing purples of the Channel meet with the whiteness of the white walls ; flaming cactuses wind their coils within the window-frames, and the fuchsia and tamarisks scarcely quiver in the breathlessness of the valleys in summer-time. Richard Carew wrote in 1602 : " The

* " Cottage Architecture," in " Memorials of Old Sussex."

ancient manner of Cornish building was to plant their houses lowe, to lay the stones with mortar of lyme and sand, to make the walles thick, their windows arched and little." In the North of England, as Mr. Sidney Jones has recently written : " Nature was in a stern mood, and the elements had to be resisted. There is a certain rugged character in the buildings, accurately representing the external circumstances and underlying powers that were continual and permanent."

Such dwellings are the abodes of the statesmen or dalesmen, as they are called, who have a history of their own worth recording. They are "statesmen," not because they have any aptitude for governing the affairs of a nation, but because they are estatesmen, or small yeomen ; and " dalesmen," not because they lived in dells or dales, but their title is derived from an old word, " delen," to divide. They divided the country amongst themselves, and each man had his own pasture-ground marked out and fenced round with rough stones. Those who know Westmorland and Cumberland are familiar with the numerous stone walls that intersect the fells and hills. These marked the boundaries of an old dalesman's holding. And there they lived, erecting for themselves scattered fell-side hamlets, bleak and bare, and attended to their flocks and herds and fostered habits of sturdy independence. Not even kings could dispute their rights, and when James I. tried to assert an imaginary claim to their lands, two thousand swords were unsheathed at Kendal with the intimation that their owners were ready to defend the lands they had preserved so long from marauding Scots. It is sad to reflect that in recent years the number of dalesmen has been steadily decreasing especially in Cumberland.

Bishop Creighton thus describes the statesmen's habitations: They were mostly built of a rough framework of wood and stone

A CUMBERLAND FARM

filled in with wickerwork, daubed with clay, and smeared with cow-dung. The chief room served as a kitchen, dining-room, and sitting-room for the family; the principal object which it contained was a huge oaken closet or press, with panels adorned with simple carving, which made a handsome piece of furniture, and passed on from one generation to another. On one side of this room was a pantry, and on the other the *bower*, or bedroom where the

37

master and mistress slept. The upper storey was a loft, without ceiling, where slept the children and servants; it was divided by a compartment between males and females. Such was the abode

NAB COTTAGE, RYDAL
(STATESMAN'S HOUSE ABOUT 1750)

of the thrifty and independent dalesman, who farmed his land and lived chiefly on porridge and milk, wove his own cloth and linen at home, and, beyond attending fairs and markets, seldom saw any one but the " butter-badger," who called to purchase his superfluous stock of butter.

Descending from these lonely hill-dwellings by ways bounded by stone walls golden brown with moss, the earth copiously besprinkled with its auburn-coloured filaments and the pale mountain speedwell, and the base bestarred with stitchwort and blue bird's-eye, the yellow pimpernel, and the deep pink flowerets of the wild geranium, we come to the valleys of the Lake District, and see trim home-steads and picturesque cottages at Grasmere and Rydal, as if made of Dresden china. We see Rydal Mount, where the most famous of the Lake poets lived during the latter part of his life, with its terrace-walks and garden-steps, the porch with its seat and the house sheltering itself beneath Nab Scar. We give a view of the Nab Cottage.

Dove Cottage, that "little nook of mountain-ground," in the vale of Grasmere, was the home of Wordsworth during that part of his life upon which imagination most fondly lingers. There he settled in 1799, and remained for eight happy years. Thither he brought his bride, Mary Hutchinson, enjoyed his friendship with Hartley Coleridge, wrote the "Recluse," the "Excursion," and many of his best shorter poems. It is a tiny house, but rich in the memories that haunt its small chambers, and is now dedicated to the poet and preserved as a national memorial to his worth and merits. Peace reigns in the Grasmere valley, a scene of quiet beauty, serene and happy.

Recollections of very different scenes go with us as we climb the fells of Cumberland. We are nigh "the Debatable Land," where the Scots and English for centuries waged a continual

war, and spent their days in raiding each other's cattle. It is a
land of Border keeps and peel-towers which tell of

> Foragers who with headlong force
> Down from that strength had spurr'd their horse,
> Their southern rapine to renew,
> Far in the distant Cheviots blue,
> And home returning, fill'd the hall
> With revel, wassal-rout and brawl ;
> Methought that still with trump and clang
> The gateway's broken arches rang :
> Methought grim features, sear'd with scars,
> Gazed through the window's rusty bars.

The Scots of Harden and other clans lived by these raids.
One Walter Scot became tired of the warfare and lazy in the days
of Queen Mary. One day on sitting down to dinner he and his
retainers, when the cover of a huge dish was raised, beheld simply
a pair of clean spurs. It was a hint from the laird's wife that
they must shift for their next meal. So Scot of Harden sounded
his bugle, mounted his horse, set out with his followers, and
returned next day " with a bow of kye and a bassen'd [brindled]
bull."

These peel-towers were raised to defend the homesteads on
the Borders from the marauding Scots, and though time has
destroyed many, many a farmstead contains the kernel of the
lower storey of a tower, around which the rest of the buildings
have been erected. The name, peel, is derived from the wooden

palisade which guarded the farm and its buildings ; but as wooden fortifications were easily destroyed by fire, the great weapon of the freebooters, stoneworks were substituted, and then a tower raised, and hence the word was transferred from the oaken palisade to the stone tower. It had a vaulted basement, which was the storehouse of the family, and above the common room of the family. On the third storey was the women's bower, while at the top were stationed the fighting men who kept watch and ward, and had a beacon ready to summon aid from a neighbouring peel. Such were the original structures. In the fifteenth and sixteenth centuries other buildings were added, a hall and solar, and some have developed into country houses with much luxury and refinement, such as Levens, Bleage, and Barton ; while others are in ruins, such as Arnside, Lammerside, and Capperside, while the majority are farmhouses and retain recollections of the sad times when fire and sword swept the country bare and famine and pestilence stalked in the footsteps of the freebooters.

As we have illustrated so many examples of timber-framed cottages it may be advisable to consider how they were formed, and to admire the ingenious art of the village carpenter who could rear such beautiful evidences of his skill.* We may notice that the old English word for to build was *timbran*, or *getimbrian*,

---

* The method has been clearly described by Mr. Charles Bailey in his " Remarks on Timber Houses," published in the Surrey Archæological Collections, and to him I am indebted for much information with regard to the architectural construction of cottages.

which means to " timber," and the builder of a house was named *treowwryrhta,* or a carpenter.* First a foundation is made of brickwork or stone on the ground marked out for the cottage. In some sixteenth-century accounts this is called " basing stone." It is usual to style these houses " half-timbered " when the foundation walls are continued to some elevation, but they are nearly all timbered houses, entirely wood-framed. At each corner a trunk of a tree was set up with its roots upwards, and these roots were carved into brackets for the support of the upper storey. Sometimes grotesque figures or carvings of saints or arms were carved upon them. On each side of the house upright posts were set up between the two corner posts and fastened into horizontal beams at the top and bottom of the face. Then horizontal beams were fastened into the corner posts and bevelled into the upright posts, and thus the framework of the side completed, a similar process being adopted on the other three sides. The next task was to fill up the interstices. Some of these were left for the windows to be fitted in and a doorway provided, and then laths were fitted into slots in the posts, and wattles or rods of hazel were woven in and out of the laths. These would scarcely serve to keep out the winds and rain. Hence they were covered over with " daub," a mixture of clay and straw or cowdung, and when dry this coating was colour-washed, usually in the South of England with a yellowish hue, or whitewashed in

* " The Evolution of the English House," by S. O. Addy.

TILLINGTON, NEAR PETWORTH, SUSSEX

NEAR the lordly Petworth, in Sussex, the seat of the Earl of Leconsfield, and formerly the home of the powerful Percys, stands the little village of Tillington, just beyond the Park of Petworth, on the road to Midhurst. It lies just north of the Downs, in a region of immense woods and heather commons and quiet country life. The cottage is characteristic of Sussex, originally of half-timber construction, and the upper storey tile-hung with red tiles of the same colour as the roof, which glow in the glory of the setting sun, while the garden is a mass of flowers which refuse to be confined within the low stone wall that guards the little domain. A giant yew guards the entrance gate, and greets the woodman returning from his work bearing logs, his lawful perquisites for his winter fuel.

GREAT COMBERTON, WORCESTER

THIS village of Great Comberton, Worcestershire, is in the beautiful Vale of Evesham, under the Bredon Hills. The hills, in a grey, sombre tint, form a pleasing background to a rich thicket of oaks that border the southern bank of the Avon near to it. The house shown in the sketch is a charming specimen of the farmhouse type. The nearness of the upright timbers of the projecting gable betoken an early date, probably the early part of the sixteenth century, the portion on the right of the picture having been added later. A pinnacle crowns the gable, the thatch boldly projecting beyond the walls, which are composed of timber, the interstices being filled with wattle and daub. The thatch is a work of art, and is made to curve gracefully over the windows of the upper storey.

Cheshire, the wooden beams and posts in the North Country being painted black. Hence the " magpies."

Amateur architects always forget something, a door or a staircase, or something quite unimportant. And being an amateur I have forgotten the roof or upper storey. Some cottages were quite content with the one storey, as are several of the beautiful cottages shown in the illustrations. The first storey was boarded over, the gables set up with tie-beams to keep the slanting pieces in place, the roof boarded, and then thatched or tiled. In order to admit light into the attic, dormer windows were added, and this attic provided sleeping accommodation for the family. An external chimney of brick was constructed on the gable end near the door, which was screened off by one of the walls of the ingle-nook.

But many cottages had two storeys, and on the framed work already constructed the builder reared the upper chambers. The beams of the floor of these apartments projected beyond the lower storey, and boards were placed on these extending to the corner posts, and on the extremities of the joists posts were erected as in the first building and horizontal timbers tenoned and mortised as before. In towns the projecting storeys, which were called " jetties," were not allowed to be less than nine feet from the ground, so that people would not knock their heads when they rode on horseback under them. The roofing, chimney, doors, and windows were added as in the one-storeyed dwelling.

# THE COTTAGES AND VILLAGE

As we have said, there is immense variety in cottage-building. Sometimes the upright posts were placed near together, as in the cottage at Chiddingstone, Kent, or in that of Great Comberton, in Worcestershire. This is an indication of early work, showing that the dwelling was constructed in the first half of the sixteenth century. The neighbouring woods supplied plenty of timber, but when this became less plentiful the posts were placed further apart, and so less timber was needed and the interstices became larger. In order to strengthen the building curved braces were added, formed of curved branches of trees cut longitudinally, and these add beauty as well as strength to the walls of the cottage. You will notice these curved braces represented in the sketches of the dwellings at Steventon and East Hagbourne, in Berkshire, and in many others.

Another sign of early work is the placing of small facing boards at the ends of the joists of the upper floor, and these were often carved and crowned with small battlements. Later on they were rounded off, as in the cottage at Kersey.

These rounded ends are much more common than the others. When any of these dwellings are pulled down it is noticed that the framework is bound together by wooden pegs. No iron nails were used. Our forefathers were cunning men and knew that iron rusted, and rust eats into the timber and tends to decay.

In order to protect the timberwalls from the weather they were often covered with tiles. Our artist has depicted several of these tile-hung dwellings, which abound in Surrey, Sussex, and Kent. Such is the charming cottage at Tillington, near Petworth, in Sussex, lying just under the noble park of Petworth House, the august home of the Earl of Leconfield. Petworth Town and neighbourhood afford a paradise of old-fashioned architecture, and this little cottage is a picturesque example. A bright sunflower raises its head in the garden, and the owner is returning homeward, wearied with his toil at the close of day, but not too wearied to carry with him a burden of logs for his winter fuel, which are the perquisites of woodmen on most estates owned by liberal landlords. We are glad that the good man has such a pleasant home. But our present interest in it is that it is tile-hung. The use of these weather tiles is not very ancient. It is an instance of the way in which our forefathers devised and thought out many inventions. The draughty and weather-worn cottages needed repair. After a century or two had elapsed since their construction they were cold and cheerless. So their owners about the year 1750 bethought them of this method, and much of the work was done in the latter part of that century or early in the nineteenth. They are the old sixteenth-century timber-framed structures in a new shell. Moreover, our forefathers realised that the ordinary tiles used for roofing were somewhat too heavy for the purpose, as these would drag at the nails that fastened them to the walls, the weight being unrelieved by the slope of a roof. So they devised thinner and flatter tiles for this purpose.

# THE COTTAGES AND VILLAGE

In some of the illustrations of the cottages our artist has depicted some that are weather-boarded in order to make them impervious to rain and wind. Deal boards were placed horizontally covering the wall-surface, the upper board overlapping its neighbour. A thick coating of plaster was also effectual for the purpose. In modern buildings plaster or roughcast is very frequently used. "When in doubt use roughcast" is the dictum of the modern architect, and the old builders did the same. As we have said, plaster was often used to coat the wattles that filled the interstices of the framework of the walls. The method was to make a foundation of interlacing briars or hazel twigs, thus forming a sort of basketwork, and then to daub over with clay mixed with straw or some stringy weed, and upon this put a thin coating of plaster, on both the inside and outside faces.* This daub gave a name to a trade, as the old rhyme states:

> The Mayor of Altrincham and the Mayor of Over,
> The one is a thatcher and the other a dauber.

The dauber or plasterer was a very skilful person, and I have told elsewhere of his art and his strivings after beautiful designs.† He and his fellows strove to make even humble cottages fair to look upon, and they succeeded, as the remains of their work testify.

* "Half-timbered Architecture of Cheshire" ("Memorials of Old Cheshire").
† "Manor-houses of England," p. 106 (Batsford).

# LIFE OF RURAL ENGLAND

They have an ever-enduring charm, and many in these restless days will echo the poet's wish:

> Mine in a cot beside the hill,
> A beehive's hum shall soothe my ear;
> A willowy brook, that turns a mill,
> With many a fall shall linger still.

# V

## BENEATH THE OLD ROOF-TREE

BE the home great or small, there is something more than sentiment that clings around the roof. It has sheltered us for years. We have watched it grow old and grey, as perhaps we have ourselves, and we think of our fathers who reared it and made the place our home. They say to us:

> We did our best for the old home,
>   We reared this roof-tree well;
> And we trust that you will be strong and true
>   To the home where we loved to dwell.

This appeals with equal force to the humble dwelling of the cottager as to the home of the squire or the mansion of the great, save that his tenure is often less secure and Octobers will come and often compel him to seek the shelter of another roof-tree. But on the estate of the old English squire labourers used to live on from generation to generation and never knew an alien lord, and son succeeded his father in the old cottage, which was as much the family home as the manor-house was that of his master.

It is the custom of English builders when the roof-tree has been reared to hoist a flag on the building to signal the triumph of the achievement. I know not how old the custom is, but it

48

has evidently come down to us from a remote past, and is still in use.

It may have some connection with the idea of a spirit haunting a house. Every self-respecting old house has its ghost, some restless spirit that haunts its ancient home of love, or wrong, or crime, and will not rest. The foundation-stones of a house were bathed with human blood by the ancient Picts. In modern times the workmen enjoy a meal consisting of bread and cheese and ale, called a *fooning pint*, when the foundations are safely laid. It is a kind of sacrifice to the ghost, and without it the inhabitants of the house will have to endure divers misfortunes and never enjoy either health or happiness. Perhaps the decoration of the rafters of the roof was intended to propitiate the spirit.

The accounts of the building of a house in 1575 show that it was "mossed" and "slated." Probably a bed of dry moss was laid down first, and this was then covered by slates. Green moss or turf was not an uncommon covering, as it was cheap and plentiful. In the North of England turf was laid on a foundation of ling or heather. But thatching * with straw on reeds or rushes is the most common, and our artist revels in thatched cottages, of which he has depicted many charming examples. The man who devised that beautiful little cottage at Midhurst was a genius, and its roof is a triumph of graceful thatching that spreads itself

* The word "thatch" is derived from the Saxon word *theccan*, to cover, from which the roof was called *thecan*.

49

over the "outshut" or "outshot," or, as we now call it, out-house, descending at the gable ends in graceful "hips," embracing the dormer window in the upper storey, and covering the porches and lattice window with its golden glory. It is called Cowdray's Cottage, as it stands in the old Cowdray Park associated with the former greatness of the Montagus. The old house is now a ruin. The curse of Cowdray descended on it, uttered by the last monk of Battle Abbey, when the ancestor of the Viscounts Montagu, Sir Anthony Browne, entered into the possession of the monastic house. The monk said that by fire and water his line should perish, a prophecy that ultimately came true, though it required three centuries to work out its fulfilment. Old Horace tells us that the high-towering pine feels most the wind's power, and though Cowdray is a blackened ruin the lowly Cowdray's Cottage remains. No curse could fall upon so sweet and humble a dwelling. The deer still roam in the neighbouring park. Here nothing ever hurries. Midhurst is a quiet country town, gabled and venerable. As Mr. Lucas tells us, "the people live their own lives, passing along their few narrow streets and the one broad one, under the projecting eaves of timbered houses, unrecking of London and the world. Sussex has no more contented town." One of the charms of Sussex is that it is so little spoilt by modern notions, and on account of its isolation it has retained so much of old-fashioned English ways. Mr. Kipling, who dwells within its borders, at Burwash, sings well its praises :

CROPTHORNE, NEAR EVESHAM, WORCESTER.

COWDRAY'S COTTAGE, MIDHURST, SUSSEX

COWDRAY'S COTTAGE is a triumph of graceful thatching that spreads itself over the " outshut " or " outshot," or, as we now call it, the outhouse, descending at the gable ends in graceful " hips," embracing the dormer window in the upper storey and covering the porches and lattice window with its golden glory. The garden is a blaze of colour. The cottage stands nigh Cowdray Park, upon which the monk's curse lies, as we have told in the text. But no curse could fall upon so sweet and humble a dwelling. It probably takes its name from the house and park upon the borders of which it stands, though some tell that its title is derived from the name of a former owner of the name of Cowdray. Its charms are characteristic of the beautiful unspoilt shire of Sussex.

God gave all men all earth to love,
  But since man's heart is small,
Ordains for each one spot shall prove
  Beloved over all.
Each to its choice and I rejoice
  The lot has fallen to me
In a fair ground—in a fair ground—
  Yea, Sussex by the sea !

The picturesque cottage at Ardington, in Berkshire, affords another example of graceful thatching. We notice the exquisitely neat finish of the roof-ridge, the most critical point of the whole, the geometrical patterns formed by the spars just below, which help by their grip to hold it in its place for years. This old cottage has climbed the bank above the roadway, so that the door has to be reached by a flight of steps, and a hand-rail assists the ascent and descent. The cottage seems to have taken refuge there to escape from the muddy road, which the traffic of ages and perhaps the action of water have scooped out. You will often find in England the roadway sunken below the level of the adjoining fields. Before it was a road, macadamised and gravelled, it was a pack-horse track. In winter a stream of water flowed along its course, and traffic and the water have worn away its surface, until it is as we see it to-day. The bank is covered with grass and foliage. The village is ancient. It was the settlement of the royal race of the Vandals, and lies just off the Roman road, called the Portway. It may be noted that villages often planted themselves just off the main roads ; you have to turn down a by-lane and travel about half a mile to reach the hamlet. This may have been planned for the sake of security, in order that, hidden amongst the trees, it might not attract the attention of lawless bands of roving robbers. We could tell many a story of outlaws and their misdeeds, of private wars and outrages that disturbed the peace of the countryside. So Ardington sheltered itself among its trees just off the main road, and there built for itself a fine church, which was rebuilt in the thirteenth century, and set up a cross in the churchyard, which is decayed, and a fine new one tells the story of the Faith which has shed its light in the old village since St. Birinus converted the pagan Vandals to the present day.

One great danger always threatened these thatch-covered houses, and that was fire, a danger that was increased by the inflammable nature of walls built of timber and wattle. Hence a large number of early cottages have disappeared. In ·order to diminish this ever-threatening danger cottages were often white-washed, and even the thatched roof received a coating. There were in those days no fire-engines ready at a moment's notice to be rushed out and dragged to the scene of the fire ; but a large number of stout iron hooks with chains were kept in readiness to pull off the thatch and pull down the timbers of the doomed cottage, so that it might not be a source of danger to its neighbours.

But other materials are used besides thatching, and next in importance and beauty as a roof-covering rank tiles. The tiler was an important person in every village community. If you examine old register books you will find that the trade of the persons named therein is often recorded, and it is not difficult to discover the principal occupations of the inhabitants, and to gather how self-centred the village was, how able it was to supply all its needs without outside help or foreign interference. And amongst the various trades that were carried on in the village we find the *tegulator*, or tiler. He made tiles very different from the modern hard-looking variety with a semi-vitrified and impervious surface, such as the Broseley tile, manufactured by machinery and never varying in tone or colour. The old hand-made tile was not always perfect, but it harmonised well with the natural surroundings, and when time and weather have worked their will upon them they assume beautiful hues of tone and colour. The tiler used to make those thin bricks which we see in mediæval buildings. In fact, a brick was called a *tigel*, or tile. It is generally supposed that the art of brick-making practised by the Romans was lost in England. We do not find the word "brick" in the books of English writers until the fifteenth century, but tiles were used, though not very generally, before that period. The houses in towns were principally thatched, and this incurred the danger of fire. Hence the authorities ordered tiles to be substituted for thatch, and when fines were levied for breaches of the regulations and by-laws the culprits were sometimes ordered to pay them in the form of tiles. Thus, at Reading in 1443 if a barber kept his shop open after ten

# THE COTTAGES AND VILLAGE

o'clock at night he was ordered to pay a fine of 300 tiles to the Guildhall. Poor John Bristow was ordered to pay 4000 tiles for disobedience to the mayor. Sometimes it was very difficult to procure this form of roof-covering. The Paston Letters inform us that in 1475 "there is none to get for no money"; and again: "Master Stoby begs loan or alms of tylle to roof one of his fayrest chambers which standyth half-uncovered for default of tylle."

The county of Worcester has many beautiful examples of tiled-roofed and picturesque cottages, especially in the villages of Oddingley, Cropthorne, Defford, and in many others. We give a sketch of the half-timbered tiled-roofed cottage at Cropthorne, near Evesham, a very old village, as it was granted by King Offa (A.D. 758–796) to the monastery of Worcester. In the parish there is the sad spectacle of a ruined chapel, that of Netherton, which dates back to Norman times and possesses a quaint tympanum, showing a dragon with a kind of flower for head and mouth, huge outspread wings, and a long tail curling well over his back. The village lies on the banks of the beautiful Avon, which William Sandys in 1636 made navigable from Tewkesbury to Stratford for boats of thirty tons burden by placing "wires" (weirs) and gates, one of these having been erected below Cropthorne Mill. The memory of good deeds lingers long in rustic minds, and old men still call part of Cropthorne Weir "Sandys' Post."

A very pretty tiled-roofed cottage is that of Small Hythe, near Tenterden, in Kent. It is entitled to fame as having been for some time the residence of the favourite actress Miss Ellen Terry. It is a half-timber construction, with nail-studded door, and stands in a district remarkable for hops and sheep. Tenterden Church raises its steeple heavenwards, and a curious legend is connected with it. Its building by the Abbot of Canterbury is said to have caused the loss of that fair region of Kent that extended eastward, and is now submerged, the Goodwin Sands being its only remembrance. The Abbot is said to have used for the purpose of building the steeple some stones that guarded the sea-wall which protected Earl Goodwin's lands from the attacks of the sea. Hence the wall gave way, the sea rushed in, and has ever since rolled over the Earl's fertile acres. There is, of course, little truth in the story, which varies much in detail. Bishop Latimer in one of his sermons attributed the silting up of Sandwich Haven to the building of this steeple.

Many curious legends cluster round our churches and hamlets. An illustration is given of the fine church on the hill at Kersey, in Suffolk. There was a priory in the village, and all that remains of it is a wall incorporated in a stable. Why was that church built on a hill somewhat far removed from the inhabitants? It may have been a pilgrim church, like St. Martha's, near Guildford, situated far from any houses, its dedication being a corruption of St. Martyr's, referring to the destination of the pilgrims who

55

trod the Pilgrims' Way on their road to the shrine of St. Thomas of Canterbury :

> From every shire's ende,
> Of England, to Canterbury they wende,
> The holy blissful martyr for to seeke
> That them had holpen when that they were sicke.

Possibly the goblin builders may have been at work, as they were at Rochdale, in Lancashire. There the church is on a hill, and the people have to climb a long flight of steps to attend to their devotions. The builders of the church began to erect the church in the valley near the houses of the town, but the legend states that every night mysterious hands removed the stones that the masons had laid during the day and transported them to the hill-top. The stones were brought back to their original position, but the goblins would have their way, and in the end the masons gave in, and the church was reared on the spot where it still stands. Legends are always interesting, and we should like to recall others, but we must return to our " bricks and mortar."

The roof terminated often in hips or gentle slopes, the tiles or thatch being extended to cover the " out-shot " or lean-to building used for storing fuel or tools or odds-and-ends. The long uninterrupted sweep of the roof and its steepness are without dormer windows or gables, signs of the early age of the dwellings. Gables with barge-boards are the usual termination of the roof, and form one of its most attractive features. Many examples are shown of these in the illustrations. There is a beautiful

Small Hythe, near Tenterden, Kent.
(Occupied by Miss Craig and Miss Ellen Terry.)

THE PRIORY, STEVENTON, BERKS

THE house known as the Priory stands on the site of a cell or dependency of the Abbey of Helloim, in Normandy, nearly opposite to the village church. It has been much restored, but still retains much of its beauty and is one of the most picturesque half-timbered fronts in Steventon, the carving on the barge-boards in the gable being very good, with pendants on either side. Formerly the house had a fine carved oak chimney-piece with figures, and the inscriptions, *Judica domine nocentes me ; Expugna in pugnantes me ;* but of this and much panelling and the old doors the house has been robbed. On the right of the house was the monks' fish-pond, which has long since been filled in. The road under the trees is called the Causeway, and runs the whole length of the village street.

projecting gable without barge-boards in the cottage at Great Comberton, in Worcestershire. It is made to project in order to protect the woodwork of the wall from the weather. A finial adorns the ridge, which came into fashion in King James's time, when pendants were also added to the eaves.

The apex of the roof is covered with ridge-tiles in the form of an inverted **V**, usually plain, but in old Devonshire houses the first ridge-tile in the main gable was very commonly moulded to represent a horse and its rider. Several of these remain, and thereby hangs a tale, the connection of the roof with the horse. The original apex of the roof was formed by two beams crossed in the form of **X**, and to prevent the top of the beams from rotting, the skulls of horses were placed upon them, partly to protect them from the weather, but principally as a sacrifice to Odin, whose grey hell-horse bears souls to the place of departed spirits Mr. Baring-Gould connects the floreated points of metal or stone at the apex of a gable with the bunch of grain offered to Odin's horse to ward off the attacks of the god of storms, and tells us that in the Black Forest farmhouses are at the present day protected from lightning by poles with bunches of flowers and leaves on the top, that have been carried to church on Palm Sunday and then devoted to their propitiatory purpose.

There is a fine example of a gable-ended house in the village street of Kersey, in Suffolk, with barge-boards. These are cut at their edges in the form of cusps, which is a sign of the early work of the late fifteenth century. Later on they were pierced with tracery in the form of trefoils or quatrefoils, and in Jacobean times by more elaborate perforated designs. This Kersey house illustrates many of the other features of cottage architecture which we have attempted to describe. It is a half-timber house, with projecting storey, a dormer window over the central bay, and with its red-tiled roof, its climbing roses, and the woods in the distance forms a beautiful picture of rural England. As in the case of the house at Great Comberton, the gable and barge-boards project from the wall, in order to protect it from the weather-storms. When in the eighteenth century houses were tile-hung or weather-boarded, this being no longer necessary, the distance between the wall and the barge-boards was diminished, and ultimately they were placed flush with it ; elaborately carved boards were discarded and the edges of the gables simply moulded. In all this we see the adaptability of the work of our forefathers to changed conditions. The walls with their new coats being able to withstand the wintry storms, projecting gables were no longer needed, and were then made to recede until they met the surface of the wall.

The gables in some of the large and important buildings in stone-yielding districts are extremely beautiful and are ingeniously devised ; and in the Cotswold region cottages and farmhouses possess fine examples. Chipping Campden is in the heart of the Cotswold, and seems to be one of the few perfect examples of the Middle Ages. It possesses scarcely a house that is not beautiful, and one of the gems of its buildings is the charming open Market House erected by Sir Baptist Hickes in the reign of James I. for the modest sum of ninety pounds. We give an illustration of this building, which affords a good example of Cotswold gables. A

MARKET HOUSE, CHIPPING CAMPDEN

pinnacle is often placed at the summit of the gable, crowned by a small globe, and adds much to its appearance. Some antiquaries see in these stone balls attached to gables a relic of the human sacrifices offered to Odin and of the human heads set on spikes affixed in pagan times when Thor and Odin were the objects of Viking worship. The heads of traitors and criminals were in mediæval times thus stuck up on spikes over city gates or town-halls as a deterrent from crime; but the authorities were only carrying on an ancient custom, the tradition of which was pre-served by the Renaissance architects, who substituted stone balls for human heads.

We have now reared and roofed our cottage. It is not very regularly built. It is not a machine-made structure, but in spite of its irregularity, or because of it, the cottage is very pleasing to the eye, and rewards us well for all our labours.

## VI

## "I'LL CREEP UP INTO THE CHIMNEY"

*—Merry Wives of Windsor*

SIR JOHN FALSTAFF was a somewhat portly person, and when in his extremity in order to escape his pursuers he proposed to seek refuge in the chimney that must have been a large and capacious structure that could have concealed his ponderous form. If we are not called upon to creep up the chimney, we can at least admire its graces. Not long ago poor boys were compelled to creep up, and endured tortures in following their trade of chimney-sweeping. Kingsley has told the story of one of these climbing boys in his "Water-Babies," and the original of his little hero is known to me. He still sweeps chimneys, but he is the respected alderman of a municipal borough, and is still a "water-baby," as he is a strong temperance orator. He has often described to me the sufferings of his early days when he was compelled to creep up chimneys by a cruel master, and his poor little arms and knees were covered with wounds and sores and had salt rubbed into them, causing excruciating agony. It was easy also to lose one's way in the complicated flues of a mansion, and death and starvation were dangers which poor climbing boys had to face. The simple chimney of a cottage home was not so complicated; the chimney-shafts are an important feature of picturesque old cottages, and form one of the chief external adornments of our houses. Modern folk are content with the erection of a little stunted funnel for the escape of the smoke, scarcely raising its shamefaced head above the hideous blue-slated roof; but our forefathers bestowed much care upon this part of their dwellings. The word itself, a chimney, literally means a fireplace, and seems to carry us back to the time when houses were warmed by the kindling of a fire on an open hearth of tiles or bricks in the centre of the chamber. As late as 1649 the hall of Richmond Palace was warmed by a charcoal fire burning in the centre of the room on a brick hearth, and having a large lanthorn in the roof for the escape of smoke. At Penshurst is the original hearth in the centre of the hall, and by its side the andirons, or fire-dogs, for arranging logs of wood upon the hearth, and over it there was an opening in the roof, with a small ornamental turret to cover it, called a smoke-louvre, but this has unfortunately been removed. However, this central hearth still remains, and it is believed to be the only existing specimen of its kind. " The custom of having a large fire of logs of wood in the hall con-tinued long after fireplaces and chimneys were used in the other chambers," wrote Mr. Parker, in his " History of Domestic Architecture," and adds: " It was a mistake to suppose that these were unknown in this country until the fifteenth century. There were many fireplaces and chimneys of the twelfth and thirteenth

THE THREE GABLES, KERSEY, SUFFOLK.

COTTAGE STEPS, ARDINGTON, BERKSHIRE.

centuries in the chambers, but it was not customary to use them in the hall before the fifteenth. In spite of all modern contrivances for warming rooms, it might be doubted whether for warming a large and lofty hall it was possible to obtain more heat from the same quantity of fuel than was obtained from the open fire, and when the space was so large, and the roof so high that no practical inconvenience could be felt from the smoke, which naturally ascended and escaped by the louvre." My old college of Oriel, at Oxford, still has its louvre, though it is now glazed and serves for the transmission of light rather than the emission of smoke.

Carew, in his " Survey of Cornwall," written at the end of the sixteenth century, states that the old builders " used to set hearths in the midst of the roome for chimneyes, which vented the smoake at a louvre in the toppe." Several old writers, however, refer to a canopy which was erected over the central fireplace and conveyed the smoke to the louvre. Leland, in 1538, was surprised to see at Bolton how " chimneys were conveyed by tunnells made on the sydes of the wauls," and the absence of the central hearth with its cover or canopy. Harrison, in 1577, wrote that " each man made his fire against a reredous in the hall where he dined and dressed his meat." This reredos seems to have been the same as a canopy.

In smaller chambers, however, the clouds of smoke would be unbearable; and " Piers Plowman " tells of the dank smoke that came from the turf fire, which could find no vent but through the window-holes and the chinks of the door, and the poor man complained that

> Smoke and smothre smyt in his eyes.

Chaucer, in his "Nun's Tale," tells of the widow's house:

> Full sooty was hir bowre, and eke hir halle,
> In which she ete many a slender mele.

However, at an early period in cottages canopies made of sticks twisted together and plastered with clay were erected over the fireplaces to enable the smoke to escape. The first chimneys were of wood, and possibly were constructed of hollow tree-trunks. It is probable that many existing cottages had originally no chimneys, as those which appear now at the end or side are obvious additions.

The chimneys of the manor-house which dates back to Tudor times, are very elaborate, with their twisted shafts of brickwork, moulded bases and ornate heads, and decorated with small panels, three shafts linked together. Evidently one of the chimneys was erected in Elizabethan or Jacobean times, as it is not so elaborate, having a straight shaft, solid, firm, and dignified, without the playful, fanciful treatment of the other. Our cottage chimneys are still less elaborate, but sometimes they approach the dignity of their more important neighbours, and are most ingeniously and cleverly designed, displaying wonderful workmanship. Plain shafts are often made most picturesque by the introduction of a number of angles in the plan, and by the projection of courses of brick, where the chimney clears the roof and at the head.

There is a very beautifully designed chimney of this nature in the cottage at East Hagbourne, in Berkshire (p. 177), with quite an elaborate head formed by projecting courses of brickwork, and another at Steventon (p. 65), in the same county.

Old customs die hard. The chimney is connected with the roof of slate or tile by what is called a flashing of mortar, and the bricklayers in Surrey used to mark this with a decoration consisting of two wavy lines with dots below and above each curve. This was made with the point of the trowel, and is a reminiscence of the old wickerwork of which houses were constructed, the dots representing posts and the wavy lines the pliant boughs woven between them. Mr. Addy, in "The Evolution of the English House," tells us that the same form of decoration is used in Yorkshire in decorating the walls of bedrooms where the walls join the slanting roof, the lines and posts being painted with a dark blue colour. It is curious that South-Country bricklayers and North-Country builders should make use of the same ornament.

Most cottages have their chimneys built at the side or gable end, and it often juts out from the wall, and is wide and deep, so as to allow for the ingle-nook in the interior, wherein our fore-fathers made themselves snug and comfortable on winter nights. Such chimneys were evidently convenient for the visits of Santa

Claus or St. Nicholas, when he deigned to visit these rural abodes. The greatest width was carried up to the height of the ceiling of the ground floor, or even higher, so as to allow for the existence of a bacon loft, wherein sides of bacon were hanged by hooks to iron ribs and smoked. Only wood fires, preferably oak, were used for this purpose.

In the West of England there are "cloam" ovens, made of clay baked hard. They are in the shape of a beehive, and carry on the tradition of the old beehive huts or dwellings which can still be seen in Cornwall, at Fernacre, and elsewhere, and are lineally descended from the first dwelling-places erected by man, the work of the Neolithic folk who raised Stonehenge and other megalithic monuments.

Our forefathers were clever enough to adapt the buildings to suit special needs. At Lingfield there is a cottage which has two chimneys that slope towards each other, forming externally a triangle with its apex at the roof, and are there crowned by a single stack. The dwellers needed two hearths and fireplaces, and by this unusual means saved the labour of building two chimney-stacks.

Some of our illustrations disclose to us the wealth of good stone-built cottages, which have some very charming chimneys retaining the old Gothic influence and details. In the region of the Cotswolds some of the best examples are found with circular or octagonal shafts. These often have an ornamental cap carved with Gothic design. They look very tall and dignified, and here again we can admire the ingenuity of the old builders. Not for beauty were they reared so high; but being very wide the down-draught was great and troublesome, blowing the smoke into the room and putting out the fire; so in order to overcome this unpleasantness the builders made them very lofty, and so added to their attractiveness.

Many examples of charming chimneys are seen in the illustrations. We may point out that simple central chimney of the cottage of Amberley, in Sussex. And here I may digress to describe the manifold interests of this little village. It is famous for its fishing, its trout having earned the tribute of praise from all disciples of Isaak Walton, who himself glorifies them. Fuller recounts the fishing farm of Sussex, and says: " Now, as this county is eminent for both sea and river fish, namely an Arundel mullet, a Chichester lobster, a Shelsey cockle and an Amberley trout; so Sussex aboundeth with more carpes than any other of this Nation." And then the old historian gives us a lengthened treatise upon the "galls of carpes" and the stones in their heads, which are " medicinable," and of the refusal of the Jews to eat caviare of sturgeon, because it has no scales and is therefore forbidden by the Levitical Law—but we need not follow him in his learned exegesis. Amberley boasts of a ruined castle or cas-tellated mansion, built by Langton, a Bishop of Chichester, in the fourteenth century. His successor fortified it with a moat.

# THE COTTAGES AND VILLAGE

It was held by Sir John Briscoe during the great Civil War, and Charles II. is said to have slept there when he was flying to France after the disastrous fight at Worcester. It is now a farm and shelters cattle. Indeed, all Amberley, according to Mr. Lucas,* is a huge stockyard, smelling of straw and cattle. " It is sheer Sussex —chalky soil, whitewashed cottages, huge wagons," and he adds that there is nothing more beautiful under the stars than a white-washed cottage when the lamp is lit.

But to return to our chimneys. There is a very fine one at Brent Eleigh, in Suffolk, composed of twin shafts, octagonal in shape, with an elaborately decorated head of Tudor design. There is a fine one at Elmley Castle, of later date, with moulded top, that adorns a very charming half-timber cottage with lattice windows inserted in the spaces between the timbers, deep thatch, and those delightful little coverings over the doors forming a miniature porch to protect a calling neighbour from the rain.

There is another good chimney at Harvington, in Worcester-shire, on the Avon, near Evesham, where the half-timber cottage-house is very picturesque with its thatch brought over the porch, and its beehives. One of these is of the modern pattern, we are glad to notice. The other is of the straw style. Modern bee-keepers do not follow the old-fashioned barbarous custom of killing the bees in order to extract their honey ; but we know some who still cling to the old traditional method.

* " Highways and Byways in Sussex."

Welford-on-Avon shows us a grand chimney with a triple shaft, each octagonal in base. The view of Groombridge Common exhibits several fine examples, all being adorned with projecting courses of brickwork, and one built against the gable end of a cottage, wide at the base and narrowing as it reaches the roof.

The drawing of Biddenden, in Kent, formerly famous for its cloth-making industry, shows a fine half-timber house with upper windows jutting out on brackets, and a good chimney. The name of this quiet and retired village, far removed from the ordinary tourists' track, reminds us of the custom of the Biddenden cakes which I have described in my book on "Old English Customs." There were two sisters, Eliza and Mary Chulkhurst, who are known as the "Biddenden maids." Some say they lived about the time of the Norman Conquest, but more reliable testimony fixes their date about 1560. Tradition states that they were the precursors of the Siamese twins, and were joined together in the back by two ligaments, and passed a joint existence of thirty-five years. One of them died, and the other refused to be severed from her dead sister and died six hours later. By their will they bequeathed to the churchwardens of the parish church certain lands, of which the rents were to be devoted to supplying the poor with doles of bread and cheese every Easter Sunday. The income of the charity amounts to about £40. Crowds flock to the village from the neighbourhood, and a kind of fair is held. After the morning service two distributions are made. A thousand hard-baked rolls, each stamped with a representation of the foundresses of the feast, are distributed among the visitors. They are very durable, as they are as hard as wood, and may be kept as curiosities for twenty years. The second distribution consists of loaves and cheese, and is limited to the poor of the parish. One of the churchwardens sits at a little window of the workhouse, and to each of the poor parishioners who march past in single file he hands a loaf and a large piece of cheese. The ceremony finished, many of the visitors attempt to soften their cakes in Kentish ale, and pass the rest of the day in old-fashioned conviviality. The Red Lion Inn and the other hostelries are well patronised, and then Biddenden resumes its accustomed quietude, as we see it in the illustration, until the memory of the twin sisters is again celebrated.* The historian of Kent, Hasted, regards the notion that the sisters were joined together as a vulgar tradition, arising from the figures on the cakes, and says that their real name was Preston. The church shown in the drawing was built in the thirteenth century, with subsequent additions. The tower is a fine fifteenth-century structure of the Perpendicular style, with battlements and stair turret. Within the church there are the remains of a rood screen.

Biddenden and its maids and cakes have drawn us away from our architectural studies of cottages, and we must hark back to the scent and hunt up the quarry. One matter I had almost

* "Old English Customs Extant at the Present Time," by P. H. Ditchfield (Methuen).

BIDDENDEN, KENT.
(Formerly cloth-making village.)

COTTAGE DOOR, AMBERLEY, SUSSEX.

forgotten in the construction of our chimneys. We must have a lightning-conductor, not a vain thing with wires and glass, but a goodly plant, the herb house-leek. If you plant this on your chimney-stack or roof you can defy the lightning—at least, if you have faith, the simple faith of a humble cottager.

# VII

## THE FOUNTS OF LIGHT AND AIR

"AND God said, Let there be light, and there was light." So it was when the worlds were framed by the Great Architect of the Universe, the first day's glorious work ; and when we frame our houses we must have light therein, the source of health and happiness, " of all material things the first and best." It seems strange to recall the time when there was a tax on the light that shines through our window-panes and cheers our hearts with its bright rays. In old farmhouses we often notice windows that have been bricked up. This was done on account of the window-tax imposed by a foolish Government in the seventh year of William III., which was not repealed until 1851, when the tax on inhabited houses was substituted for it. Houses were taxed according to the number of windows they possessed, a rough-and-ready method of determining their size and importance. Hence people shut out the light of day from their dwellings by sealing up as many windows as they could spare. Mediæval cottages had no glass in their windows. Only wealthy folk could afford this luxury. In churches glass was used, wonderfully stained with representations of saints and martyrs and of Him who was worshipped therein.

72

# COTTAGES OF RURAL ENGLAND

From the passage from "Piers Plowman" already quoted we gather that the smoke from the hearth found its way out of the cottage through the window-holes, the chinks of the door being an additional outlet. Glass was scarce in the Middle Ages, and when Richard II. wanted some for the repair of the windows at the chapel in Stamford he ordered Nicholas Hippeswell to scour the four counties of Norfolk, Northamptonshire, Leicestershire, and Lincolnshire to obtain the necessary material and "to take as much glass as he could find."

Glass, however, came into fairly common use in Tudor times. In small farmhouses and in some cottages a window with a cusped head of true Gothic character is sometimes found. We have seen one in the White Horse Vale in Berkshire, at Ashbury, which was formerly a monastic grange attached to the Abbey of Abingdon. In stone districts two or three lights were placed together, divided by moulded mullions and having one drip-stone over them. The manor-house of this period had a large bay window at the daïs end of the hall, and when the house has lost its ancient dignity and become a farm or been converted into cottages this feature remains. In the Cotswold country we find the old grey stone-built, gable-ended cottages of infinite variety, erected by men of traditional taste, who did the right thing because they could not help doing it, and the windows of their dwellings constitute one of their chief beauties. Sometimes windows, called oriel windows, jut out from the wall, supported by brackets; and dormer windows break the surface of the roof. These were needed to give light to the upper chamber, the floor of which was very little below the eaves of the roof. We know a cottage where the upstairs room has no dormer window and its lower sill is flush with the floor, an exceedingly inconvenient arrangement for lighting the chamber. Moreover, the ceiling was so low that my friend, who happened to be a tall man, was obliged to stoop when he entered his bedroom and could never raise his head to his full height. In the steep-sloped roof of a cottage much space was naturally lost in the upper part of the house, and when numerous children, like the olive-branches, were gathered round the owner's table, requiring more sleeping accommodation, he would utilise what we call the attics, construct some chambers therein, and secure light by constructing little dormer windows entirely in the roof. Many of the illustrations show examples of dormer windows, some built up above the wall of the cottage, and others nestling in the thatch. Several picturesque dormers are seen in the sketch of Groombridge Common.

In timber-framed houses it was not difficult to insert windows in the spaces between the upright and the horizontal timbers wherever light was wanted, instead of the wattle and daub that filled in the other interstices. The ingenious way in which these were fashioned, the art shown in their construction, and the beautiful effect which they produce have been admirably depicted in our artist's drawings. Sometimes we see graceful bay windows jutting out from the side of a cottage. These are usually additions, and mostly date from the time of Queen Anne.

Great skill was exercised in the glazing, plain, small, lozenge-shaped leaded panes being the most common in old-fashioned cottages. They were in use in the time of Shakespeare, as is evinced by his statement in his play "All's Well":

So, my good window of lattice, fare thee well ! *

The lozenge-shaped pieces of glass are set in leaden glazing, and this is inserted into iron casements. Much skill and ingenuity were expended in the construction of the uprights and handles, which are often of very beautiful design. There is a house at Guildford, in the High Street, now a shop, where there is a very large number of these window-fasteners, all different in shape and pattern, the handiwork of some skilful and ingenious smith. Many cottages have been shorn of their old lattice windows, and have received instead of these the less picturesque square or oblong panes, or the comparatively modern sash window. The best of the old work has too often been destroyed. A pretty lattice window is shown in the cottage at Bignor (p. 17), in Cowdray's Cottage at Midhurst (p. 51), in the cottage at Selworthy, Somerset, and in many others.

There is a charming little oriel window supported on brackets in the almshouses on Selworthy Green (p. 78), having lattice

* Act ii. sc. 3.

windows and a thatched covering. It would be difficult to imagine a more pleasant retreat for old age than these delightful dwellings with beautiful gardens, wherein the flowers grow as if they wished to cheer the eyes of the aged inmates, to comfort them when age and infirmity had left their marks upon them, and to tell them of the fairer garden of Paradise whither their Maker was leading them when earth and earthly things had passed from their sight. Old almshouses are often a distinctive feature of villages. They were erected usually by some squire who wished to benefit the old people on his estate, and endowed them with lands and money so that they might last for ever. Of these the poet sings:

> Oh, the good old times of England!
> When her gentlemen had hands to give and her yeomen hearts to feel;
> And they raised up many a bede-house, but never a bastille;
> And the poor they honoured, for they knew that He, who for us bled,
> Had seldom, when He came to earth, whereon to lay His Head.

The door is a very important feature of the house, and tells of many happy comings and goings, and of some sad ones too. There the mother stands waiting to welcome her young children back from school. She is blest with many olive-branches, but a little later on she told me: "When they are young they make your arms ache; when they are older they make your heart ache." Poor mother! may that not be their common lot and experience. Through that door the labourer home returns weary with his daily toil, saying to himself:

GROOMBRIDGE, KENT.

DOVE COTTAGE, GRASMERE

To the lovers of literature and the admirers of Wordsworth Dove Cottage will always have an ever-enduring charm. The scenery around it inspired some of his sweetest songs.

All the things the poet held dear are there—"the flowering shrubs that deck our humble door," bright gowan and marsh-marigold, flower and weed from distant mountains, primroses, and even a sparrow's nest.

> O happy garden ! whose seclusion deep
> Hath been so friendly to industrious hours !

So the poet sang his sweetest lay, when he was about to bring his bride to this fair bower, and the echo of his song still haunts the house and garden that he loved.

Be the day weary, be the day long,
At length it ringeth to evensong.

And great joy reigns when a soldier son from India enters through that door, and brings with him presents from that far-distant land, and tells his wondrous stories and adventures ; or when a daughter who has married returns home for a holiday, bringing two tottering youngsters who are the pride and joy of their grandparents.

The door and the threshold are very sacred. It is not well to stumble at the threshold, as Shakespeare, who knew his folklore, tells :

For many men that stumble at the threshold
Are well foretold that danger lurks within.

In olden days it was protected. A sacrifice was made when the threshold was laid. Amongst many peoples it was customary to sacrifice a calf or a sheep, or a hen, or a cock, and bury it beneath the stone in order to keep out evil spirits. The remains of animals so sacrificed have often been discovered beneath the thresholds of old houses. Witches used to be a great trouble to us, and we have scarcely yet ceased to believe in the power of the evil eye. Mysterious diseases carried off those who had incurred the wrath of a witch. Hence in order to prevent these old beldames from injuring us we still hang up horseshoes on our doors ; but it is very important that the points should be upwards ; otherwise they are of little use for keeping out witches. It will also be quite as effectual if we bury beneath the threshold bottles containing nails or pins. When a bride comes to her new home she should be carefully lifted over the threshold; otherwise ill-luck will befall her. Perhaps the cause of the custom of leaving open the door of a cottage may be traced to the traditional belief in the benevolent action of the good fairies, who used to perform all manner of kind actions for the housewife. They would churn the butter and do many other pleasant little " odd jobs." Certainly it was not an uncommon practice to leave a hole in the wall for the " piskies," or pixies, to come in and out as they pleased.

Lest we become " pixie-led," a dangerous form of letting one's wits go wool-gathering, let us look at the door itself. If it is old, it is probably made of oak and studded with nails, like one of the doors of the cottage at Small Hythe, near Tenterden. Sometimes there is a thumb-latch. The string-latch, which Red Riding-Hood was directed by the wolf to pull, has departed; but we have stayed in an old abbey which has been restored by its present owner, who has introduced the string-latch for all the inner doors of his house; and it works admirably. At night many of these old doors were fastened by a heavy wooden bar passing across their whole length and fitting into holes in the walls of the house. Even the poor cottager was not always safe from midnight marauders and the lower ranks of highwaymen, and a good stout bar gave a sense of security. If we are in a stone-bearing district we shall find many good doorways which retain Gothic features.

The arch is fashioned in the Tudor style and has moulded sides and a hood-moulding.

On the door-post of a cottage I have detected a little votive cross rudely carved on the moulded timber. It is not usual to find such inscribed on the door-post of a domestic dwelling, though you may see many on nearly every mediæval church, if scraping and restoration have not removed these tender memories of simple faith. It was not unusual for a man when about to undertake a journey to scratch or carve a little cross on the stone or woodwork of his church door, at the same time registering a vow that if his life were spared and he was permitted to return to his home in peace and safety he would make some offering to God who had preserved him. Such crosses were called votive crosses. But they are seldom seen on cottage door-posts, and possibly this moulded beam may have been brought from the neighbouring church during some of those terrible " restorations " which are so destructive to the ancient features of our ecclesiastical buildings.

In the region of good stone-quarries the doorway is fashioned very carefully and well of good wrought stone. It looks almost as grand as the fine doorway in the church, but is not quite so marvellously wrought. That was fashioned by the Norman masons, who carved such strange designs on the tympanum, the meaning of which no one can quite determine. The rector of the parish is a very learned person, and he can tell you about most things in and out of the village. I am not sure that he is always right, but neither rack nor thumbscrew would ever force me to dare to dispute his statements. But even the rector is puzzled by that curious design. It shows a tree with branches covering the whole surface, and two weird-looking animals are nibbling at the branches. We ventured to suggest that this represented the Tree of Spiritual Life and Knowledge, and that the animals represent all creation seeking life and salvation from the wondrous Tree, the leaves of which are for the healing of the nations. The rector disputed this, but I believe it to be correct, notwithstanding his refusal to accept this solution of the problem. I should like to tell you of other Norman doorways, of the recessed sides with their two or three orders, the finely wrought arch, of the shafts with their capitals that form the sides, and of the amazing number and variety of these carved tympana.* You may learn much from the imagery and symbolic lessons conveyed by their rude carvings. Thus, over a Norman arch we often find a row of curious, hideous bird-like heads with beaks. These are called " beak-heads," and were doubtless intended to represent the " birds of the air " in our Lord's parable of the sower, which were ready to dart down and pluck out the good seed that had been sown during the service in the church, from the heart of the faithless or indifferent listener. Very demoniacal they look, these impish birds, a terror to the weak,

* Mr. Charles E. Keyser has made a special study of Norman tympana and visited nearly every church in the kingdom where one exists. His researches have been recorded in his book on " Norman Doorways and Sculptured Tympana " (Elliot Stock).

unstable minds who have allowed the golden words of truth to fall in vain.

Sometimes cottages possess these fine old Norman doorways. At Sherborne, in Gloucestershire, a cottage has one that was brought from a disused chapel. It has a chamfered hood-mould adorned with pellets and saw-tooth, zigzag and chevrons. Beak-heads, too, appear at the sides, and there is a shaft with a scalloped capital, and a tympanum with a plain Maltese cross in the centre and another more ornate cross on either side. The same cottage has another Norman doorway at the back. It is perhaps hardly fair to this cottage to disclose these relics of Norman builders, as I expect collectors and architects will sweep down upon it and carry off the doorways. I will even venture to describe another cottage that boasts of a Norman doorway. It is at Buckland Fields, in the same county of Gloucester, and the very beautiful doorway is said to have been brought from the destroyed church of Laverton, and is now built up in a wall of the cottage. A monster head with tusks looks down from the apex, and below it are arches formed of a series of bold angle zigzag, rows of pellets and other carvings of an exquisite character, and a plain tympanum.

But such doorways are exceptional. They are not the natural entrances to a sixteenth-century cottage, and we prefer the more homely and picturesque doorways which are shown in the illustrations, protected by a rustic porch with seats on either side, or simply by a wire or wooden framework that has been covered by vine-leaves, or clematis, or other pleasant creepers. The porch is part of our scheme of garden culture, and must be left to our gardening chapter and not trespassed upon here. Our best plan is to admire some of these beauties which the artist has displayed, and then enter the cottage by the inviting door, if the good woman will permit, to see and to investigate her few treasures, prized by her with quite as much satisfaction and keen sense of ownership as are the costly paintings, gems, miniatures, or Sèvres by the millionaire.

# VIII

## HEARTHS AND HOMES

THE peasant housewife is a very kind and gracious body, sturdy and independent, who will welcome you with all the graces of a duchess to her humble dwelling ; but if you are foolish, superior and patronising, and, still worse, very curious, the cottage door will perhaps be shut when next you are pleased to call, and you will not be able to buy " for an old song " those charming pieces of Staffordshire ware wrought in curious figures, nor add to your collection of old furniture that delightful little escritoire that had been in the cottager's family for years. True it was very battered and worm-eaten ; but it could be easily renovated. However, it is no good—you will not get it. You have offended the old lady by your behaviour, and all the king's horses and all the king's men will not force her to part with her treasures to you. In future it is well to remember that poor people have feelings, very proper feelings, and good manners too, and to ride roughshod over them is not altogether wise, prudent, or seemly.

The old dame who welcomes you at the door has reached the autumntide of life. " It is toward evening and the day is far spent." She has brought up a large family, who have started well in life and are doing well. She has known what hard work meant, when she helped her husband to earn money to bring up the children by herself working in the fields. These rustic women are a fine race. They have often very tender souls in coarse bodies, wide, weather-reddened faces, not ill to look upon, calm, passive and veracious as the fields. It is hard work trimming swedes for sheep, picking up potatoes, going among the mangolds with skirts and sleeves sopping wet, the muddy soil clinging to everything. It is hard work, but it has its compensations. The air is bracing and health-giving. Passing one's days in the open air beneath the broad sky, witnessing the constant changes, the warm sunshine of the hayfield, the stern desolation of miles of snow, life becomes a very real thing. Hysteria and sentimentalism cannot live in such an atmosphere ; and our friend could tell us that she has never had time for such nonsense. She has had troubles—very great they have been, and would have crushed many who have not been brought up in her school. But she has triumphed over them, or rather borne them very bravely, and she is a real picture of a peasant woman, not one of those feeble caricatures which artists love to paint of lamblike old imbeciles with snowy caps and amiable smiles which are supposed to represent our peasant women.

Her husband, too, is a fine specimen of an old labourer. He can tell you many stories of the past life of the village, of the hungry times of the Crimean War, when wages were low, when

THE CHURCH GATE, WELFORD-ON-AVON, GLOUCESTER

THIS second view of Welford shows some of its characteristic cottages, and the old lych-gate, or " gate of the dead," where the bodies of the defunct villagers rest ere they are borne to their last resting-place in God's hallowed acre. The spring-blossom is on the fruit-trees, and the cottagers have found some space by the road-side for their flowers, which impart colour to the scene, and the blooms of spring-time waft a joyous message across the road to the old lych-gate, telling of life and resurrection.

A BY-LANE AT HOUGHTON, SUSSEX

JUST beneath the Sussex Downs and the shade of Bury Hill is the little village of Houghton. Houghton Forest was a region of dense woods which supplied plentiful timber for the construction of such cottages as these which stand in a by-lane, along which perhaps Charles II. and his faithful companions passed during the flight from Worcester to Brighton, whence he set sail to Fécamp. These cottages are old enough to have seen the king as he rode past across the Arun stream to Amberley. The scenery shows the character of the old forest district, with its grand old trees and " the green of the bracken amid the gloom of the heather."

bread was two shillings a gallon, when he scarcely knew the taste of meat, and he was half starved and his father could not provide loaves enough for the family. He can remember the times of agitation and feverish unrest, when men's passions were aroused, and crowds of angry rustics scoured the country breaking the new-fangled machines which they imagined would take the bread out of the mouths of their wives and children. Those were the days of rick-firing, and he remembers seeing many a farmstead blazing, many a home made desolate by the blind fury of an enraged people. He can tell you of the old popular belief in the power of witches and of the " evil eye," and of the " wise men " who could counteract their evil influence, discover tools that had been lost or stolen. His back is bowed and he suffers severely from rheumatism ; but he is very patient. As old age comes on it seems to bring with it a child-like piety which enables him to face death unmoved and to bear suffering with unmurmuring patience.

With the permission of our aged friends we will glance round their pleasant dwelling. Opposite the entrance doorway is the wall of the ingle-nook, trying to keep out the draught, and assisting to make that snug retreat warm and comfortable. A beam runs along the top of the fireplace, stretching across the opening, from which a short curtain hangs. Among the cottager's treasures we notice an old Toby-jug showing an old-time farmer decked out in knee-breeches, long-skirted coat, and three-cornered hat, his hands affectionately holding a foaming jug of ale which he regards with intense satisfaction. And beside Uncle Toby repose a milkmaid and her cow, two figures seated on a horse going

INTERIOR OF A SURREY COTTAGE

to market, and another showing the couple returning home again, a Highland shepherd and shepherdess, a little house with blue roof and scarlet door and green steps leading up to it, a big cat with green eyes, and a spotted dog of the spaniel breed. Great ladies have often attempted to persuade the old people to part with these treasures; but all in vain their offers. These nicknacks are to the cottager what Old Masters are to millionaires, and he will stick to them as long as he lives and bequeath them to his heirs as priceless possessions. An old sampler hangs upon the wall, the work of the old dame's mother when she was a child. It shows a picture of a house with trees, worked in coloured wools, with the letters of the alphabet and the maker's name inscribed, with the date. There are pictures, too, six little prints of the Prodigal Son, the figures being attired in eighteenth-century dress, and some " made in Germany " of Scripture subjects, such as the Presentation of Christ in the Temple, St. Thomas, or of mediæval legends such as the Coronation of the Virgin, or a representation of the Blessed Trinity, the Father being shown as an aged man. Sometimes these are mixed with hunting scenes, " from scent to view," and photographs of the family. Sometimes one meets with rare treasures. I have found in cottages three Bartolozzi's coloured engravings, which have been presented to me, and I prize them very much for the sake of the givers.

Dealers often systematically visit our cottages and carry away with them any old furniture they may find, giving, like the old magician in " Aladdin," new lamps for old ones. But sometimes an old mahogany chair may be discovered much the worse for wear, but of such good, sound workmanship that it has survived the ill-usage of many generations. The old man courteously invites you to sit in a charmingly inviting arm-chair. It is made of oak and has curved horizontal arm-rails, perpendicular rails, and nicely curved back, with a wheel-shaped ornamentation. There are two or three rush-bottomed chairs, a plain deal table and oak form, whereon the children used to sit when they were at home, and, of course, the seats on each side the ingle-nook. Hanging on the walls are two or three sets of brightly polished brass ornaments which were used for decorating horses and were fastened on the strap that connects the collar with the belly-band. The designs of these are various and intricate, some crescent-shaped, others like bosses with pierced patterns, such as a crown or a star, or a shield surrounded by concentric circles of pierced holes. Our host was a carter and took a great pride in turning out his team well, especially when he went to market ; and they used to have bells attached to the harness and ear-caps of bright colours, and he never took his team to the nearest town on market-days without plaiting the manes and tails with red ribbons, and the horses were as proud as Punch as they marched soberly along, and you could not have found a better turned-out team in Berkshire.

You must not forget to admire the cottage dresser and rack with the dame's clean crockery displayed upon it. It is not very choice ware, only plain willow-pattern plates and cups and saucers ; but there is a fine old china teapot that came from a big house, and was given to her by her mistress when she left service to be married. If you are very friendly she will perhaps invite you to have a cup of tea out of this choice vessel, which is only used on special occasions ; but you must be prepared to see her take out of it, before the tea is made, a packet of snuff, two or three cough-lozenges that have seen better days, a packet of needles, and a few other unconsidered trifles.

Some old tools are standing in the corner of the cottage.

FIREPLACE IN SURREY INN

Perhaps you may imagine that the new-fangled agricultural implements have quite supplanted the old tools which our fore-fathers used. Not a bit of it! They are there to-day. New things come, but the old do not pass away. The reaping-hook endures. It is an enlarged sickle which is as old as the Romans, who used to cut off the ears of the wheat and leave the tall straw standing. The sickle had a fine toothed edge which acted like a saw ; but the reaping-hook is as sharp as a razor, or nearly so, and you must keep it sharp by the use of a whetstone. There is also, there in the corner, a fag-hook which has a step just below the handle, so that the blade and the handle are on a different level. This enables you to cut hedges or brambles without skinning your knuckles. We have no time to describe the different ways of using these tools.

The flail, too, survives in spite of the yearly visits of the threshing-machines to our farms, when " the wail of the winnow'd corn " is heard throughout the village. The old flail was in use throughout all the winter, and provided work for the labourers in the dull, wet, dark days when little farming work can be done. It is one of our oldest tools, and its name comes to us through the old French word *flael*, the German *flegel*, from the Latin *flagellum*. I need not describe its construction, as the implement is doubtless well known to you.

But I have not described half the contents of the homestead— the old linen-chest, the salt-box, the knife-box, the warming-pan, snuffers, reed-holders, which tell of the primitive mode of lighting adopted by our fathers, who dipped reeds in tallow and used them as primitive candles. There is much else to describe, but the old clock is striking and tells us that it is time to leave the cottage. We admire the deep tone of its bell. It is a fine old " grandfather,"

ALMSHOUSES, SELWORTHY GREEN, SOMERSET.

FARMHOUSE, BRENT ELEIGH, SUFFOLK.

THIS farmhouse at Brent Eleigh, in Suffolk, is a little gem of the humbler forms of domestic architecture. It is a timber-framed structure, the interstices being filled in with brickwork arranged in herring-bone fashion. The nearness of the uprights indicates early work and proclaims its date about the early portion of the sixteenth century. We notice the projecting upper storey, the old door, the very fine chimney composed of twin octagonal shafts, with an ingeniously contrived and graceful head formed of projecting courses of bricks which are arranged with angular projections, the gable with barge-boards not flush with the wall, an indication of early work, and carved with cusp ornamentation.

and was made by John Hocker, of Reading, who was apprenticed to John Martin and then to Edward Joselin, and became a member of the Clockmakers' Company in 1729. It has only one hand, and has to be wound up every night; and the interior cogwheels are not very evenly cut, so that some hours pass more rapidly than others, as all hours do when you spend them in rustic cottages and hear what the peasant folk have to tell of the stories of the past. The making of these old clocks was a local industry, and the face bears the initials of the maker, "J. H.," and the place where he lived. Solemnly this ancient piece of mechanism ticks in its panelled case:

> Ninety years without slumbering,
> Tick, tick, tick!

The interior of the yeoman farmer's homestead reveals much more comfort, and is almost Dutch-like in its simplicity and homeliness. The floor is flagged with stone, the wide chinks being filled with hardened dirt. The table stands on a piece of carpet and before the vast fireplace there is a hearthrug. The shelf above bears more treasures than those possessed by the cottager; but the yeoman likes, too, the odd figures in crockeryware. Perhaps this affection for such things is instinctive and hereditary, and may have come down from Roman times when the Lares and Penates, the household deities, were worshipped by the pagan folk. Certainly the housewife loves her treasures, and on this shelf repose also old-fashioned brass candlesticks, a snuff-box and tobacco-dish. Hanging on the wall is an old-fashioned fowling-piece which once had a flint lock, but it has been converted into a gun that is discharged with the aid of a percussion-cap. Dried herbs, too, hang on a nail beside the fireplace. They are useful as household medicines.

I expect Granny's cottage on Henley Common, near Midhurst, is full of all kinds of little treasures. It is situate in a region in the rich, wild district around Midhurst, where gorse-bushes grow and great commons stretch, and hills and downs and vales extend themselves far and wide in a delightful sequence. Henley itself stands perched upon a hillside through which the old coach-road ran, sorely trying to the horses and perilous to passengers. But it has now been diverted and goes along Henley Common, whereon stands Granny's cottage, a creeper-clad, thatched, and tile-hung dwelling, with garden-path paved with Horsham slabs, and a garden rich with flowers and cabbages that flourish well, tended carefully by the old woman's hands. Here we may well linger for a while ere we embark upon the next chapter, and study more carefully the contents of the cottage garden.

# IX

## 'MIDST FRUIT AND FLOWERS

MANY of our illustrations reveal to those who are ignorant of our English country life the beauties of our cottage gardens, which form so charming a feature of our rural homes. English villagers are very proud of them, and prize their plants and flowers. In that unhappy exodus which occurs soon after Michaelmas, when labourers often leave the village and migrate elsewhere, they usually take their pet flowers with them ; and those who come to us do not fail to bring theirs too. The poor man as well as the rich loves the plot of ground he has cultivated and made beautiful, and that which we work with our own hands we prize more than that which is fashioned by a host of gardeners. Sir William Temple, who was a great gardener, wrote : " In a garden has been the inclination of kings and the choice of philosophers, so it has been the common favourite of public and private men, a pleasure of the greatest, and the care of the meanest, and, indeed, an employment and possession for which none is too high or low."

When strangers visit our shores and travel along our country roads one of the first sights that give them pleasure is that of the flowers that bloom in the wayside cottage. Look at those charming little gardens at Bossington. They are a blaze of colour and a constant delight to their possessors. There are hydrangeas, fuchsias and geraniums, lilies and begonias, and of course old-fashioned roses. That other garden at Selworthy, in Somerset, is no less delightful, with its tall hollyhocks and giant pæonies growing wild in their luxuriance, set against as quaint a cottage as you could desire, with its lattice windows and thatched roof.

The cottager has many difficulties to contend with. When he has a wife "like unto a fruitful vine," and many olive-branches round about his table, he has to be careful lest his love of flowers should trespass upon the ground that has to provide his crop of vegetables. But he has learnt to make the best of his opportunities, and that is the secret of success both in gardening and in life. As a garden, it may seem poor when compared with that of the rectory or manor-house. The cottager has often to struggle with poor soil, unless his employer is a kind-hearted man and presents him with a load or two of manure now and then. Road-scrapings in the country form an indifferent supply of nutriment for the soil. But sometimes the unnurtured earth of a cottage garden seems to impart to the tulips that flourish therein a certain slender, high-stemmed grace that is lacking in more favoured beds. One of our greatest gardeners, the late Dean Hole, said : " Every labourer should not only have this bit of brightness about a house, which looks so bare and cold without it, and should be taught to appreciate and to maintain its beauty, but to combine also that which is good for

94

food with that which is pleasant to the eye, the kindly fruits of the earth in due season. He should have apple-tree, plum-tree, and cherry-tree, his bushes of gooseberries and currants, his potatoes and greens, in addition to his garden of flowers. He should refresh his mind with the ornamental, and his body with the useful, not imitating the rigid economy of one of our Nottinghamshire squires who, being asked why he no longer kept deer in his park, replied: ' They clip no wool.' "

With all due deference to the Dean, I have not found that labourers need much teaching in order to appreciate the beauty of a garden. It seems instinctive, at least with the better sort, and they do not need the stimulus of a Cottage Garden Horticultural Show to make them care for that little piece of God's earth which for a time they can call their own. Shows, too, sometimes lead to dishonesty, and very often to jealousies and heartburnings, as every one imagines he ought to gain the first prize.

Let us look more particularly at this little garden. Usually it is confined, as we have said, to the strips on each side of the path leading to the door. It is the home of many old-fashioned plants, such as pinks and larkspurs, sweet-williams, wallflowers, Canterbury bells, and white Madonna lilies. I was permitted to transplant quite a large number of these beautiful lilies last autumn from a cottage to the Rectory garden, and they will make a brave show this summer.

The garden is guarded by a hedge of holly, which is always

welcome with its solid masses of dull, deep colour and its whole-some look of perfect health and vigour. It is a faithful guardian of this charming plot of ground, impervious to attack, ever presenting among its scarlet berries the sharp points of its prickly leaves. Holly, too, tells of Christmas, when sprigs of it are cut to adorn the pictures and walls of the cottage, and festoons of gay-coloured paper hang from the ceilings, and the squire's servants' hall is brightly decorated, and the village choir is expected to visit the manor-house and sing some such strains as

> God bless the master of this house,
>   And the good mistress too,
> And all the little children
>   That about the table go.
> I wish you a merry Christmas,
>   And a happy New Year,
> A good fat pig in the larder
>   To last you all the year.

Yes, the old holly-tree has some very happy associations. May they never die away! And as we walk up the little path and enjoy the scent of the roses and lilies and mignonette we approach the porch. It is of rustic woodwork, and is covered with a mantling vine. Cottage gardens preserve the tradition of the outdoor cul-ture of the vine, which formerly flourished throughout England. Most of our monasteries had vineyards, but perhaps it might have been regarded as a monkish penance to drink the wine that was made from the grapes grown in them. At Abingdon, in

Berkshire, where once a famous abbey stood, there is still a street called the Vineyard, which marks the site of the precincts of the monastery where the monks grew their grapes. Some cottages can boast of gigantic vines, but the grapes grown on them, save when an exceptionally bright summer comes, are seldom eatable and not very delectable. A good tart can be made of them, and the villagers manufacture a species of grape wine which vies with the various decoctions brewed by industrious housewives. There is a great variety of these beverages prepared from recipes handed down from our grandmothers. There is a cowslip wine, a somewhat sad liquid; black-currant tea, or wine, as it is sometimes called; elder wine or tea; and rhubarb wine, which is said to be equal to champagne when properly prepared. These are some of the contents of the countryman's cellar. But he prefers himself his glass of ale, or in the West Country his cider, to these fancy drinks, which he usually leaves to his womenfolk.

The rustic porch is often clad with ivy or a climbing rose, or clematis, and the walls of the cottage are clothed with creepers, roses, or ivy. Some villagers devoted to horticulture build for themselves little greenhouses, and work wonders in the production of geraniums and fuchsias and other plants that need some protection from the cold blasts of winter. Plants are like animals, and respond to the affectionate regard of their owners; and the cottager is devoted to them. An old Berkshire dame said that she could gaze at them all day long, if she had no work to do. " They be sa wunnerful, an' there is sa much in 'um. As for hurtin' or breakin' a flower, well, there, I couldn't do it ; 'twud sim downright cruel." The gardening Dean notes that the window garden is generally filled with geraniums, fuchsias, musk balsams—we have noticed also hydrangeas, begonias, and cactus—" so highly esteemed that they are often permitted to monopolise the light, and so carefully tended, watered and washed, that their growth and efflorescence are remarkable." In the summer these treasures are set to bloom afresh in the open air, so that they may make fresh growth and gain strength.

Have we exhausted the beauties of the cottage garden ? Not yet. There are still some attractions to be recorded. The garden has often a little orchard attached to it, or fruit-trees growing amongst the cabbages and potatoes, and our artist has depicted some of these when the apple-trees are in bloom, than which there can be no prettier sight. Pear-blossom, cherry-blossom, make the garden gay and bright, and we trust that no cold winds or late frosts may come to blight the prospect of a good fruit harvest. " God tempers the wind to the shorn lamb," and often in the sheltered garden of a cottage the fruit sets and grows and ripens far better than in the more exposed rectory pleasance, and brings grist to the labourer's scanty store. In an Oxfordshire village we wot of the lanes are all lined with cherry-trees which are the property of the inhabitants, who can gather as much fruit as they please.

Cottages at Dunster, Somerset.

ELMLEY CASTLE, WORCESTER.

Such country customs and the possession of a good garden which will produce vegetables for the whole year for the rustic family, and provide interest and employment in the evenings, and a perpetual delight to the agricultural labourer, make country life far better than the lot of those who have to live in towns. Our wages seem lower than those of the artisan, but we have to pay little or no rent. Sometimes we get our milk-supply free of charge, and wood can be obtained for nothing, and kind folk have left money for charities to supply a good store of coal for the winter, and we have extra money during the harvest, and some do piece-work and can earn a good wage. I have lectured and talked with the men in the East End of London, and they have told me how much they wish they were back again amidst the green meadows of their native shire, and how hard life is amidst the wilderness of bricks and mortar. But we have no use for town folks in our country. They are useless kind of creatures. They may think themselves very clever and smart, and they can talk; but of what use are they when they try to plough a furrow, or milk cows, or thatch a rick or manage a reaper? They cannot do these things. They are sort of feckless folk; and when good gentlemen in London talk loudly of " Back to the land " we know they are talking foolishly and ignorantly, and are not worth arguing with.

But we are wandering away from the garden, and there are just a few beauties that have not been noticed. One of the illustrations, the cottage at Norton, near Evesham, Worcester-shire, shows a clipped yew cut in the shape of a peacock with a long flowing tail, and there is another similar figure in the garden of a cottage in the neighbouring village of Hurst. Sometimes the outside hedge is clipped and trained so as to form a capacious covering to the entrance gate, and holly-trees cut in the form of ascending globes. Such fashions were copied from the formal garden of the neighbouring squire, or were started by an ex-gardener of some nobleman who loved to clip his yews in the form of giants and knights and birds and beasts and other strange creatures. They are out of place amidst the simplicity of the cottage garden.

The water-garden is a charming feature of a squire's pleasance. It cannot always be had, but rich folk will spend large sums of money to obtain a supply of water in order to construct an aquatic garden. Many cottages have a natural water-garden which is far superior to the artificial product. Look at those beautiful cottage gardens at Lake, near Salisbury, by the side of the sweet Avon River. Flags and water-lilies, water-plantains and the flowering rush have made their homes in the bed of the stream or on the banks, and the ducks swim about and add life and animation to the picture.

Cottage gardens produce not only plants that are fair to look upon, but herbs that are useful for the cure of all kinds of simple maladies, especially when they are used in faith. It is the cottager's medicine-chest ; and country folk are great herbalists.

An old man and his wife at Bucklebury, in Berkshire, supply a herb doctor in London with numerous medicinal plants. Tansy tea is recommended for rheumatism, the countryman's greatest curse ; marshmallow poultices are a sure cure for wounds, and white lily root ointment for gatherings. But the universal panaceas for all the ills that flesh is heir to are wood-sage and horehound. These cure all kinds of complaints, if you can believe in their efficacy. Faith plays a prominent part in all cures. We hear much of faith-healing and Christian Science. These old-fashioned remedies require faith too ; but there is certainly virtue in them. An old pensioner in my parish, who was wounded in the Indian Mutiny and bore bravely the effects of his wounds until his dying day, used to collect sundry herbs and simples and wondrously relieve the pain. It was in winter that he suffered most, when the herbs refused to grow.

"Flowres of Lavender do cure the beating of the harte," an old receipt book tells us. "They are very pleasant and delightful to the brain which is much refreshed by their sweetness. Good housewives always have lavender not only for nosegays and posies, but for linen and apparel." Warts can be cured by cutting slits in a stick of alder, or by making holes according to their number in walnut leaves. The walnut leaves must be buried secretly or put down a well. As the leaves decay the warts will vanish. I have known a man at Reading who could cure warts by his touch. He said it was a special gift vouchsafed to him by the

Almighty. A friend of mine had from childhood a wart on his hand. He went to this Reading tradesman, who after applying his finger to his mouth touched the wart, and after a second application it entirely disappeared. Another way of curing warts is to prick them with a pin, which you must then stick into the bark of an ash-tree and repeat the rhyme :

> Ashen-tree, ashen-tree,
> Pray buy these warts from me.

The ash and the maple are wonder-working trees. They will give long life to children who are passed through their branches. Cowslips will cure paralysis, and are sometimes called in the country " palsy worts," which accords with the notions of old medical writers, who termed these lovely flowers *Herba paralysis*.

With real reluctance we must leave the pleasant paradise of a little cottage garden and try to find other treasures of village life, wandering away into fresh fields and pastures new.

## X

## "'NEATH THE SHADOW OF THE CROSS"

THE artist has depicted for us several beautiful examples of old village crosses, which still adorn many a churchyard or market-place. Some of them date back to early Saxon times, on the steps of which the early missionary or Saxon priest stood when he proclaimed the Gospel message, ere churches were built for worship. The pagan Saxons worshipped stone pillars ; so in order to wean them from their superstition the Christian missionaries erected these stone crosses, and carved upon them the figures of the Saviour and His apostles, displaying before the eyes of their hearers the story of the Cross written in stone. The North of England has many examples of these crosses, some of which were fashioned by St. Wilfrid, Archbishop of York, in the eighth century. When he travelled about his diocese a large number of monks and workmen attended him, and amongst these were the cutters in stone, who made the crosses and erected them on the spots which Wilfrid consecrated to the worship of God.

I have already described in other books these early preaching crosses,* and the many charms of the English village which have

* "English Villages," pp. 95–101 (Methuen and Co.).  "Vanishing England," pp. 282–305 (Methuen & Co.).

# THE COTTAGES AND VILLAGE

matter ; or the bailiff of the manor would summon the yeomen and labourers to this place of meeting to disclose to them some order of his master.

These village crosses are very attractive and beautiful, as some of our illustrations show. They vary very much in different parts

CASTLE COMBE, WILTS

of the country and according to the period in which they were erected. The earliest are simple crosses with steps, and later on they had niches for sculptured figures.

On an earlier page will be found a description of one of those crosses that have been covered in so as to provide shelter for the market-folk, that at Dunster, and other beautiful examples may be seen at Salisbury, Malmesbury, Chichester, Somerton, Shepton Mallet, Cheddar, Axbridge, Castle Combe, South Petherton, Banwell, and other places. It is curious to note that most of these are confined to Southern England. The hardy Northmen, the Yorkshiremen and Lancastrians, seem not to have minded the rains and storms.

Many of these crosses have been ruthlessly destroyed. The Puritan faction vented their rage against them and deemed that they savoured of superstition. Hence fanatical crowds used to wander about the country, break the beautiful stained-glass windows in the church, and smash off the heads of the village crosses. Hence in many cases the cross is only a cross in name, and an obelisk has supplanted the Christian symbol. In place of this an orb has been sometimes substituted, as a mute assertion of the supremacy of the Crown over the Church ; and on the top of the orb a small Latin cross was placed ; and later on the orb was banished and a large crown supplied its place. Many crosses have disappeared in populous places during the eighteenth and nineteenth centuries for utilitarian reasons, as it was considered that they occupied too much space in the centre of the town and interfered with the traffic.

Near the cross stood the rude instruments of justice, the stocks and whipping-post. The culprit, when confined in the stocks, used to sit on the lowest step of the cross, and you will often find that this seat is considerably worn away by the many unfortunate beings who have been compelled to endure that punishment. An example of the contiguity of the stocks with the cross is seen at Ripple, in Gloucestershire, of which we give an illustration. It was certainly no slight penalty. A distinguished modern artist who loves to paint monks in various positions, such as catching fish on Thursday for the Friday's fast, used to take about with him his favourite model, and when at Sulham, in Berkshire, he placed him in the stocks and painted a picture of him. The poor man was never so stiff or so uncomfortable in his life; and

CROSS AND STOCKS, RIPPLE, GLOUCESTER

when we add to the pain caused by the strained posture the malicious torments of the crowd, the occasional throwing of stones, or rotten eggs, or refuse, the jeering and the taunts, we may imagine that an hour in the stocks was no small punishment.

We have told of the Dunster market cross, but that favoured little town can boast of two others, which testifies to the piety of

COTTAGES AT LAKE, NEAR SALISBURY, WILTS

A WATER-GARDEN is a much-sought-after adjunct to a squire's pleasance. These cottages at Lake, near Salisbury, on the banks of the Avon stream, have a natural one, wherein flags and water-lilies, water-plantains, and flowering rush have made their homes in the bed of the stream, and the ducks swim about and add life and animation to the picture. There is nothing very distinctive about the cottages. They are but humble one-storeyed dwellings roofed with thatch, which curves gracefully over the windows that shed some faint light into the rooms beneath the spread of the roof. In such rooms the lower sill of the window is on a level with the floor and serves only to make the darkness visible.

GRANNY'S COTTAGE, HENLEY COMMON,
NEAR MIDHURST, SUSSEX.

the good people of the little town in former days. In the church-yard there are the remains of a fine thirteenth-century cross having a circular base, which is characteristic of the work of the early part of that period. A small part of the shaft remains, and the head has vanished owing to Puritan iconoclasm or the action of time. Another cross in the Somerset town belongs to a different species. It is the wayside or weeping cross, and was intended for purely devotional purposes; as an old writer states, " Quersoever a cross standeth there is forgiveness of payne." This is also set forth in the work " Dives et Pauper," printed at Westminster in 1496.

Such was this third Dunster cross. When pilgrims passed along the road they would stop and pray beside the cross, and the poorer persons would sometimes find alms left there for them by richer folk. In the days when churches were few wayside crosses, too, were used as resting-places for funeral processions. There were no hearses in mediæval days, and often the coffin had to be borne a considerable distance. Hence the bearers were not sorry to find frequent resting-places, and the hearts of the mourners were comforted by constant prayer as they passed along the long, sad road with their dear ones for the last time. At each a prayer for the soul of the departed was offered or the *De profundis* sung.

Many of these wayside crosses have disappeared, as in the earlier days they were thought little of and supplied the farmers with convenient gate-posts. The Dunster cross is a good example of fourteenth-century work. It is now headless and raised on steps, and there are certain holes in the shaft which probably supported the image of some saint. Another Somerset cross of which we give an illustration is that at Crowcombe, a very graceful example of the fourteenth century. The steps are much worn by

CROWCOMBE CROSS, SOMERSET

the feet of many pilgrims, and the shaft is crowned with a Greek cross. It is situated in the middle of the roadway, at the entrance to the quaint little village of Crowcombe, which nestles so prettily at the base of the Quantock Hills.

Two of the illustrations show Berkshire crosses. One is at East Hagbourne, where there is a second cross and the base of a wayside cross in a hedge. It is one of the most picturesque villages in the country, a true example of the old English type, full of old half-timbered cottages, some of brick set in zigzags, and some with tiled roofs which stand out well against the background of fine trees. It is naturally a favourite haunt of artists. The cross forms the foreground of as beautiful a picture of an English village as one would wish to see, while behind it stands the fine and noble fifteenth-century church, with massive Perpendicular tower, on which is a beacon turret intended to guide travellers who might have lost their way in the open country. You can see, also, on the tower a very perfect sanctus bell-cot, pinnacled and foliated, whence the little bell sounded forth its sweet notice to the villagers when the Host was raised at the celebration of the Mass, bidding them, though engaged in their daily tasks, unite in heart and will in the service of the sanctuary. There is much to interest us within the church, wherein we can find the work of the early English builders in the chancel blended with that of the masons of the fifteenth century. Curious carvings, old stained glass of the fourteenth century, brass memorials of former bene-factors, all add interest to this grand old church.

The cross itself has high calvary steps formed on a square base, and is probably of the same date as the church; but it has lost its original head, which has been replaced by a shaft piercing three globes. The cube on the top of the shaft is doubtless original and may have been carved with figures of the Saviour on the Cross, St. John, and the Blessed Virgin; but some one has placed on one side of it a sundial. A stream runs through the village, formerly known as the Hacca-broc, whence the place takes its name.

The other Berkshire village of which we give an illustration is Long Wittenham. Its name carries us back to Anglo-Saxon times, and signifies the home or enclosure of Witta. It has been known as Earl's Wittenham, and also Wittenham Abbots, as it once belonged to the priory of Longueville Giffard, in the diocese of Rouen. It is an instance of the continuity of a village site dating back to prehistoric times. Many flint implements have been found, the relics of Neolithic man. The Romans or Romano-British folk had a settlement here, and when Witta came with his Saxon followers he established his abode and called it Wittenham. There is much to see that is good in this pleasant Berkshire village —a fine church of fourteenth-century date which has a curious and quite unique piscina that combines the hollowed-out stone and drain for cleansing the sacred vessels after the Communion service and the founder's monument. This is a small cross-legged effigy of an unknown knight. Perverse people continue to assert that he must have been a Crusader, but it is well known that the fact that the figure is cross-legged bears no such signification. And then we examine the cross that stands where the main roads meet. It has been much restored, but it forms a beautiful feature of the old village, and tells of the piety of its people.

Leaving the delectable county of Berks, we proceed to the ever-interesting region of Evesham, which abounds with historical associations that cluster round its old monastery and a battle that was fought in the time of Henry III., when Simon de Montfort was slain :

Salve, Symon Montis-Fortis
Totius flos militiæ.
Duras pænas passus mortis
Protector gentis Angliæ.

Everywhere in the old town there are grand old buildings, such as the Bell Tower, almost the only relic of the past beauties of the Abbey, Abbot Reginald's Gateway, the two churches with their architectural gems of chapels with the fan-vaulting ; but we are searching for crosses, and not far away is Childs Wickham, a picturesque village which has an old cross, but the head of the cross has been destroyed, and an urn now crowns the structure. It forms a pretty group with the church behind it, its fine spire pointing heavenwards, whispering a *Sursum corda*. Childs Wickham has been built on the banks of a stream, and if we wander along its course northwards we come to another Wickham, known as Wickhamford, which has a good church and contains a monument that always interests our American cousins when they are pleased to visit us. It marks the resting-place of Penelope Washington, a member of the same family as the great George Washington, first President of the United States of America. The tablet bears the Washington arms, the stars and stripes which are believed to have been the origin of the national flag of the New England States. The following is a translation of the Latin inscription : " Sacred to the memory of Penelope, daughter of that most distinguished and renowned soldier Colonel Henry Washington. He was descended from Sir William Washington, Knight, of the county of Northampton, who was high in favour with those most illustrious princes and best of kings, Charles the First and Second, on account of his gallant and successful military achievements both in England and in Ireland : he married Elizabeth, of the ancient and noble stock of the Packingtons, of Westwood, a family of untarnished loyalty and patriotism. Sprung from such famous ancestry, Penelope was a diligent and devout worshipper of God ; she was the great consolation of her mother (her only surviving parent) ; to the sick and needy she was an exceptionally ready and generous benefactress. Humble and chaste, and wedded to Christ alone, from this transitory life she departed to her spouse, February 27, Anno Domini 1697." All epitaphs are not to be entirely trusted, as the little girl seemed to realise when, after reading several, she asked her mother : " Where are all the bad people buried ? " But doubtless Penelope was a noble and distinguished gentlewoman, worthy of her illustrious kinsman.

Returning to our crosses, if we motor from Evesham to the famous Abbey of Tewkesbury, five miles from the former, we come to a turn that takes us to Ashton-under-Hill, where we find a well-preserved village cross in a very pretty village. It has a square base with a calvary of three steps, and an octagonal shaft which is

COTTAGE GARDEN, SELWORTHY, SOMERSET.

BOSSINGTON, NEAR PORLOCK, SOMERSET.

now crowned by a sundial. An illustration of this beautiful cross and its surrounding picturesque Gloucestershire village has been given by our artist.

In the market-place at Middleham, in Yorkshire, there is a curious stone which teaches the same truth which the presence of the cross inculcates. It consists of a platform on which are two pillars. One carries the figure of some animal in a kneeling posture. The carving is rude and the identity of the creature can only be conjectured. It is either a sheep or a cow, and the other supports an octagonal object traditionally supposed to represent a cheese. The farmers used to walk up the opposing flights of steps when concluding a bargain, shake hands over the sculptures, and the bargain was made and could not be afterwards broken.

We have recorded several kinds of crosses, but our list is not exhausted. Crosses marked the boundaries of monastic estates and also of counties. The estate of the Hospital of St. John of Jerusalem at Oldham was bounded by seven crosses. At cross-roads crosses were often erected, and suicides were buried there with a stake driven through their bodies to prevent their ghosts from walking, and perhaps to beseech the merciful pity of Him who once hung upon the Cross. At holy wells there were crosses in order to wean those who sought their aid from superstitious thoughts and pagan customs. In old days criminals could seek sanctuary at certain churches and religious houses, and remain there in safety, but if they strayed beyond the precincts marked and religious act to build a bridge, and frequently some hermit was entrusted with its care and maintenance. Hermitages were erected along the great highways, and especially at bridges and fords, for the purpose of assisting travellers. In the pictures of St. Christopher we often see a lonely hermit holding out his torch or lantern to light the giant ferryman as he transports his passengers across the dangerous ford by which the hermitage was built. If we were travelling in mediæval times through dense forests and approached an unknown ford, the sight of the light in the hermit's window and the sound of his chapel bell would be grateful and comforting. He lived on the charity of the passers-by, like George Pratt did at Bow Bridge, and sometimes he was authorised to levy tolls (*pontarium*) on all passengers for the repair of the bridge. The reparation of roads and bridges was also considered part of the work of the clergy. Travellers were considered unfortunate folk and needed pity; so the Church took compassion on them, and guilds and brotherhoods were founded for their maintenance and reparation. Roads were dangerous, and the passage across fords after much rain when the rivers were in flood often resulted in death by drowning. If the river was broad and deep there would be a ferry, and the ferryman had to be paid for his trouble in taking passengers across the stream. A monkish rhymer in 1416, at Abingdon, tells sad stories of the dangers of Culhamhithe (ferry) at Abingdon, when " cartes and cariage were marred in the myre," and poor folk caught cold or " payed of their purse," and beggars were

refused passage. " Culhamhithe hath caused many a curse,"
he tells us, and

> Another blyssed business is bigger to make
> That there the pepel may not passe after great schowres,
> Dole it is to draw a dead body out of a lake
> That was pulled in a fount stone * and a fellow of owres.

The old bridges were built to please God and to help His
poor. There was on the Continent a special religious Order
called the Pontife Brothers, for the making of bridges, and in
England private charity has accomplished the same good work.
Bishop de Kellawe of Durham early in the fourteenth century
granted forty days' indulgence to all who will draw from the
treasure that God has given them valuable and charitable aid
towards the building and repair of Botyton Bridge. Similar
indulgences were granted to those who helped to make the bridge
and highway between Billingham and Norton, and the causeway between Brotherton and Ferrybridge. Those who laboured
with their hands or helped with their purses were entitled to the
indulgence. We repair our roads and keep our bridges in order
by levying rates which people grumble at and are compelled to
pay. Just as the Poor Rate is a poor substitute for a voluntary
and charitable gift, so the charity and pious offices for the reparation of highways and bridges lose that religious character which
rendered self-denial popular when converted into a compulsory
rate.

* *I.e.,* baptized in a stone font.

# THE COTTAGES AND VILLAGE

Sometimes a great merchant would have his goods damaged when passing a ford, and he would build a bridge for his own advantage and the good of his fellows ; or a queen would get a " ducking," as did Queen Matilda at Stratford-atte-Bow—where Chaucer tells us the pronunciation of the French tongue was not exactly Parisian. So she built two bridges there, and endowed them with the proceeds of some land and a mill, entrusting the charge to the Abbess of Barking.

" Piers the Plowman " enjoins merchants to build hospitals, repair " wikked ways " or roads, and to " amende brygges to-broke by the heye weyes." As M. Jusserand tells us, " the pious character of the bridges was also shown by the chapel that stood on them." On the old bridge at Caversham, near the Berkshire town of Reading, there was an ancient chapel. In 1239 Engelard a Cyngny was ordered to let William, Chaplain of the Chapel of Caversham, have an oak out of Windsor Forest with which to make shingles for the roofing of his chapel. Passengers made offerings in the chapel for the repair of the bridge and the maintenance of the chapel and priest. It contained many relics which were eagerly seized by Dr. London, the King's Commissioner, at the time of the dissolution of religious houses. Of course this old bridge has disappeared, but it existed until 1870, when a modern erection was substituted for it. It is extremely ugly, but is certainly more convenient than the old narrow bridge which satisfied our forefathers.

Some of these bridge chapels still survive, such as the very beautiful decorated building at Wakefield, on the bridge across the Calder, dedicated to St. Mary. It was built and endowed by King Edward III. There are also chapels on the bridges at Bradford-on-Avon, St. Ives, Huntingdonshire, and one "of stone wel wrought" (as Leland records) at Rotherham, in Yorkshire.

These bridges were also strategic points in military campaigns. To be able to hold a bridge over a river that could not easily be crossed except by a *détour* of several miles was a distinct advantage. Hence not a few fights and skirmishes have taken place on bridges. On the old Caversham bridge a severe engagement took place in the time of the great Civil War. During the Wars of the Roses a battle was fought on Maidenhead Bridge, and at Radcot Bridge, in the same county, the Dukes of Derby and Gloucester fought against the favourite of Richard II., Robert de Vere, Earl of Oxford, and compelled him to seek safety by plunging his horse into the river.

These bridges were built fair and strong by English masons who knew well the secrets of good building, and constructed them so surely and so well that many mediæval bridges still survive to delight us by their good masonry, massive piers, their fine arches and cut-waters, their low parapets gracefully curved with moulded coping-stones, and the singular-looking triangular resting-places that break the surface of the upper masonry. In remote parts of the country, away from the great cities and manufacturing centres, many of these old bridges remain undisturbed by any considerable growth of traffic that requires a wider roadway and more convenient thoroughfare. Many of them were doomed to destruction by the greed of monastery-wreckers and the covetousness of Henry VIII. As we have said, many were supported by endowments. Pious folk had bequeathed lands or houses for the support of a bridge-guild, to provide the stipend of a priest to say masses for the souls of the founder and his relations, and to keep the bridge in repair. But the greedy king confiscated all guilds that could conveniently be deemed in any way connected with superstition; hence the money that ought to have gone to the upkeep of the bridge disappeared also into the coffers of the king.

Sometimes the repair of bridges was kept up by tolls demanded from passengers, and the right of collecting tolls (*pontarium*) was eagerly sought after by corporations and by individuals. Tolls were often levied on the owners of barges or vessels passing under the bridge, as well as on passengers going over it; and the persons who received the tolls were very glad to pocket the proceeds, but often forgot to do the necessary repairs. But the king's justices were empowered to survey bridges, and if the persons liable for the repairs failed to execute them when required they rendered themselves liable to the seizure of their goods.

Happily, in spite of the neglect of the proper protectors of bridges, in spite of the destruction wrought in modern times,

NORTON, NEAR EVESHAM, WORCESTER

THIS cottage at Norton, in the Vale of Evesham, shows a remarkable triumph of topiary art, a yew-tree cut into a series of ascending globes and crowned by a peacock. The cottager is very proud of this ornament to his garden, and also may well be satisfied with his charming cottage with its neat thatch. In the distance is Norton Church, a very interesting building, said to have been originally erected by Abbot Brokehampton about the year 1290. It is dedicated to St. Egwin, and has a remarkable marble lectern of twelfth-century workmanship, bearing the saint's effigy in the act of blessing, and holding a pastoral staff surrounded by scroll-work.

LILAC AND APPLE BLOSSOMS, HARVINGTON, WORCESTER

HARVINGTON, in Worcestershire, is on the Avon River that flows through Stratford, and is associated with sundry schemes for its early navigation, a lock having been placed there below the mill. This is a simple cottage by the wayside, sketched in the spring-time, when the apple-trees and lilacs are in full blossom. There is nothing very remarkable about the little house, which is of half-timber construction and thatched, of not very early date, as the large panels indicate. The housewife wears one of those charming old-fashioned white bonnets which are not very common now, and has been feeding her fowls. Cottage-bred fowls are wonderful layers, probably because they receive more care and attention than in a large farmyard.

we have many beautiful examples of the art of bridge-building, especially in country byways, along the roads that led to important monasteries and the ivy-clad ruins of mediæval castles. Wales can boast of many fine structures, such as the four-arched four-teenth-century one at Llangollen. Durham has two Norman bridges. Hereford can boast of a fifteenth-century one of sixteen arches.

We give an illustration of a picturesque bridge at Allerford, Somerset, which spans a stream where formerly there was a ford. Its ruined cut-water tells a tale of neglect and demands attention ere the rude floods of winter bear down upon it and sweep the whole structure away. It looks very beautiful when the summer sun is shining against the background of dark trees. At Coombe Bissett, near Salisbury, there is a gracefully curved bridge leading to the village, with the church in the distance, forming a pretty group of peaceful English village life.

In Northamptonshire, the county of "spires and squires," where good building-stone has enabled the masons to accomplish so many triumphs of architectural skill, there are many rivers, and yet being small, the

Golden streames so interlaceinge the cheareful Hills and Dales,

naturally induced the formation of bridges, instead of depending on fords, which were liable to high floods. Here and there Edwardian masonry may still be traced in the arches. Ditchford and Geddington, where stands one of the few remaining Eleanor crosses, are good specimens of fair-sized bridges with several arches and prominent cut-waters, built beside and coexistent with the old fords. They are just wide enough for one vehicle. Of a great age and pointing to the anxiety of our forefathers to keep their merchandise dry is the old pack-horse bridge at Charwelton, in which the Cherwell takes its rise, and its first bridge is this at the entrance to the village, consisting of two pointed arches and a cut-water with parapets at each side, giving width for both foot- and horse-passengers. Unfortunately it is now dwarfed and blocked up considerably by the modern construction carrying-road. Though generally considered to be of the middle of the thirteenth century, it would appear likely to date from the York and Lancastrian wars, when the road from the Midlands to London turned through the village from Church Charwelton, and eventually became one of the great highways of the coaching era.* Tockingho Bridge was widened from a pack-horse structure. There was a very narrow bridge at Eddington. Lord Cardigan, who would travel very fast in the old days of post-horses and stage-coaches, arrived at this bridge and discovered a waggon slowly wending its way across it. He shouted and swore at the postboys and made them gallop through a deepish ford beside the bridge.

A Shropshire squire made a wager that he would ride from London to his home in a certain number of hours. He was

* " Memorials of Old Northamptonshire," by Miss Dryden.

accomplishing his journey with satisfaction to himself when he came to a bridge and found to his disgust that the central arch had been carried away by a flood, and a huge gap yawned between him and his home. To cross the river by another bridge would have entailed a long *détour* and lost him his wager; so with consummate courage he set his horse to leap the wide gap, and cleared it in safety. A broken bridge was a serious obstacle in the days when such structures were few and far between. In war-time bridges have been intentionally cut through in order to hinder the advance of an enemy. One of the arches of the bridge at Wallingford was so broken in the time of the Civil War, and you can still detect the part which was so cut through.

That is a picturesque little foot-bridge near Porlock, in Somerset, which we have already visited, crossing a stream the banks of which have a wealth of flowering plants and rushes, and near it is a group of picturesque cottages. Many foot-bridges are not so secure as this one, which is of stone, some consisting of a single plank and a hand-rail, upon which if you lean it is sure to collapse and land you in the river. We remember a slight wooden foot-bridge that spanned a North-Country stream that was wide and deep. The hounds were hunting; puss crossed in safety, and also the hounds; but the riders were " held up." However, a young schoolboy, the son of the vicar, riding a little pony and wearing a smart coat made out of his uncle's (an Admiral) uniform, rode up, boldly crossed the bridge, and hunted the hounds himself.

# THE COTTAGES AND VILLAGE

The squire was furious, and said the boy must go to a public school, as there was no knowing what he might do next. The boy's courage enabled him to hunt lions and discover the Victoria Falls.

Oftentimes you will see an old ruined bridge, possibly of Roman origin, alongside a mediæval one, but quite detached. But when, as at Bradford-on-Avon, the old narrow pack-horse bridge was too narrow for the wains of the clothiers, they built in James I.'s reign a second bridge close up to the first, and spent two hundred marks in the work of reparation, and made a structure which it is always a delight to behold.

Nothing can be more beautiful in our old-world towns and villages than these ancient bridges. They are " things of beauty and a joy for ever." Some have the base of a cross where pilgrims used to worship, and as we gaze at the river from the low parapet we love to look upon one of the fairest scenes of England, the tall and graceful banks of trees, the little path that runs along the side of the stream where some happy urchins are trying to fish, the river with its banks lined with rush and bulrush and white lilies spread themselves on the surface of the water ; and the stream flows placidly along and makes no impression on the boldly projecting cut-waters. For centuries the stream has been flowing under that bridge. The monks came and leaned over this same parapet as we are doing to-day, enjoying the sunshine and looking for a trout. Armed warriors clad in steel fought fiercely on this narrow roadway, and the stream ran red with the blood of horse and rider. Queen Elizabeth rode across it with a gay cavalcade on one of her Progresses, when she was on her way to visit my Lord Burleigh or Sir William Fitzwilliam or Sir George Fermor, or other notable subjects, who did not always appreciate the somewhat costly honour of a visit from the restless Queen. We see the visions of these various personages reflected in the water, and we wonder what other scenes the old bridge will witness, whether a foreign conqueror's foot will ever tread upon it and rude war disturb the peace we prize. But it is time to pass on our pilgrimage and leave the old bridge to its musings and its fate.

## XII

## OUTLAWS AND MOATS

PEACEFUL England—though whether it is now entitled to retain that epithet is a little doubtful—was at various times in its history anything but peaceful. There have been wild outlaws in our forests such as Adam de Gurdon and Richard Siward—*cum multitudine armatorum*—revolting peasants, intent upon equality and loot, nocturnal raids by armed neighbours who held opposing political opinions, or, deeming "the law an ass," preferred to wage a private war and settle disputed questions of ownership by the might of their own right arm. All these were disturbing elements in a peace-loving countryside. Hence it was that farmers and squires were obliged to surround their houses with some means of defence, and a good wide ditch or moat admirably served the purpose, a lasting monument murmuring of the insecurity of days long dead. Crenellated mansions and castles, the abodes of chivalry and feudalism, were going out of fashion when the Tudor manor-house with its guarding moat, sole protection against troublesome visitors, came in. And yet they were only the first line of defence. A gate-house with a useful protecting portcullis, as at Hever Castle, still frowned down upon the traveller who craved admission ; but it was only a mild sort of frown, nothing very severe or alarming as in the olden days of fortress-building. But within them were cunningly devised traps for the unwary, certain masked doorways dark and obscure, whence a sword-thrust or dagger might dart forth to the undoing of a traitorous guest, and, as at Ightham Moat, a convenient oubliette outside the door of one of the fairest chambers in England, by means of which the said traitorous guest might quickly find his way into the moat and never be heard of again in the land of the living. More-over, in troublous days, when people were liable to arrest on account of their religious or political opinions, it was necessary to provide means of escape or concealment when soldiers came in overwhelming force and resistance would be useless. Hence the house would be provided with secret chambers and hiding-holes, wherein the victim of persecution might lie concealed until the danger of arrest was past. Curious hidden ladders sometimes led from the secret chamber to an underground passage which conducted the fugitive to a convenient distance from the house and permitted him to emerge in safety. Especially are these contrivances noticeable in houses that have been owned by recusants, by the adherers of the " Old Religion " who had refused to conform to the tenets of the Reformers. In this book we are dealing principally with the cottages of England and village life, and are not concerning ourselves with the stories of manor-houses and mansions ; but moats often surround the dwellings of cottagers or small farms. In this parish in which I am writing, near the church there are two conjoined cottages surrounded on three sides by a fine moat wherein rushes grow and ducks disport themselves, and on the edge of it some years ago a silver groat was found. I expect that these cottages were fashioned out of a substantial farmhouse, the owners of which thought that they would sleep more securely in their beds if they possessed a guarding moat.

It speaks ill of the peace of this district of the Old Windsor Forest to have to record that in this same small parish there is, or rather was, another moated house. It was a farmhouse, called Bigg's, which was pulled down a few years ago, and the moat is scarcely visible; but in order to preserve its memory I have christened the new substantial little mansion erected on the site the "Moat House."

As late as two centuries ago these moats were needed in this Windsor Forest district. The country was wild and open, and there were daring gangs of ruffians roaming through the neighbourhood, robbing parks and fish-ponds, and demanding money, regardless of all authority. Wild deer roamed the forest; these they captured by means of a hook fastened in a tempting apple, or shot with their guns. These lawless desperadoes were called "Blacks," and their practices were known as "blacking," because they used to black their faces when engaged in their marauding expeditions. Their lawlessness passed all reason. Gilbert White,

THE CROSS, EAST HAGBOURNE, BERKSHIRE.

On the Avon, at Lake, near Salisbury.

in his " History of Selborne," wrote : " All the country was wild about deer-stealing. Unless he was a hunter, as they affected to call themselves, no young person was allowed to be possessed of manhood or gallantry." Led by one William Shorter, the Wokingham Blacks were a terror to the neighbourhood. Lord Arran, at Bagshot, killed some of their dogs, and they threatened to come and burn down his house. Sir John Cope sentenced one of their number, and awoke next morning to find five hundred pounds' worth of his young plantations destroyed. They threatened to burn the house and farm of one Nunn, an under-keeper of the forest, and shot bullets into his chamber in order to force him to pay five guineas and to give them a buck, repeating the attack on other occasions. Magistrates were intimidated. A poacher was captured, his guns seized, and a fine of £10 levied. The unfortunate churchwarden who received the money was compelled to hand it back by threats of arson. The Blacks visited a keeper's house, maltreated him, and would have shot him, but the guns aimed at him flashed in the pan. His young son, however, who put his head out of a window to remonstrate with the gang, was shot dead.

We need not follow the doings of these lawless bands, who continued their misdeeds until the Black Act was passed in 1723, and four of them were hanged in chains on Bagshot Heath, and others transported. There are spots near our village which the rustics used to pass with a shudder, and avoid altogether if they could, when the moon shone on a loathsome gibbet, and winds caused the chains that held the gruesome remains of a highway-man, sheep-stealer, or " Black " to rattle, and restless ghosts seemed to haunt the air. Thither a century ago a solemn procession had marched, the prisoner dressed in mourning in a cart

THE FORTIFIED END, OLD SOAR, KENT

draped in black, followed by his sorrowing relatives. Javelin-men guarded the cart, and in a coach came the sheriff and chaplain. Then the gibbet was set up and the wretched criminal delivered a speech which he had carefully prepared in order to make " an edifying end," standing in the cart with a rope round his neck. Then the end came, and the crowd would wait to see the body cut down and dressed in chains to be re-hung.

It is no wonder that in the lawless condition of the old forests the good farmers and squires were glad to defend their homes from robbers and marauders. We give an illustration of the fortified farmhouse of Old Soar, in Kent, and of the kitchen of the house. Cottagers, too, had their defences. The upstairs

THE KITCHEN, OLD SOAR, KENT

room was reached by a ladder, at the top of which there was a heavy trapdoor. When this was banged down on the head of an intruding robber and kept closed by the bulky weight of the cottager and his portly spouse, it offered a sturdy resistance to the enemy. But the squires and farmers usually surrounded their homesteads with the watery guard of a moat. A bridge connects the little island-home with the world. Formerly it could be raised and lowered at will ; but the chains are rusty and the wheels have gone, and the bridge is a permanent structure now or replaced by a causeway. No troublesome visitors are expected now, unless a foreign enemy comes to invade our shores, against whom the best of moats would offer but a feeble defence. In summer-time when the sun shines and gleams through the trees that stand on its banks, upon its still waters, and ducks sport on its surface, the moat appears a charming feature of the farm or cottage home ; but it makes the house damp and cheerless in the dull winter days, and we wish it were drained and turned into a garden. However, the moat tells of times of storm and stress, of fight and foray, of crime and lawlessness, that have long since passed away, and makes us thankful for present peaceful days which we trust no bugle-call to arms, no internal strife and unrest will ever disturb.

# XIII

## IN MART AND HOSTEL

In olden days the village was very self-centred. It was more or less independent for its supplies on the outside world, save that the pedlar used to bring his pack to ply his trade and persuade purchasers to buy by his fluent tongue and merry jests. The chapman was a very welcome person in olden days, as, besides his wares, he brought news of the great events that were going on in the kingdom when intercourse between town and village was restricted and communication difficult. He carried a wonderful assortment of goods in his pack—pins, points, vests, girdles, hats, caps, laces, gloves, knives, glasses, tapes, and much else. He was an itinerant shop, and when shops were few and far between his calling was a very useful one. Even still we meet him occasionally in our country lanes ; but he is sad-faced and slow of speech, a mere ghost of the merry Autolycus who plied his trade a few centuries ago, and whose portrait Shakespeare has painted for us.

But by degrees shops began to be set up in the hamlets and village, and the shopkeepers prospered as they suffered little from the stern competition that now threatens their successors. No tradesmen's carts from the neighbouring town invaded the precincts of the village. The turnpike gates prevented them from interfering with the custom of the village shopkeeper, as the cost of the toll would have increased the prices. The hamlet had its own black-smith, butcher, cordwainer, mason, &c., was quite able to fend for itself without any interference from outsiders, and the shop was the general "supply stores" of the village. Though its custom is some-what interfered with by such modern innovations as co-operative stores, or the so-called International Stores of the market town, and by the aforesaid tradesmen's carts, it still exists and provides most of the goods a rustic requires. The old shop is a half-timbered structure, but some one in the days of Queen Anne has added an attractive bow-window for the better display of the commodities.

There is an old shop at Lingfield, in Surrey, a very interesting building, which has been admirably described by Mr. Charles Bailey in his "Remarks on Timber Houses." * A brief account of this I have already given elsewhere,† but will venture to allude again to this notable instance of a venerable shop, as such examples are rare. You can see the corner and upright posts with their projecting brackets, and the ends of the girders and joists, standing out and supporting the upright quartered sides of the upper storey. The spaces are filled with bricks placed "herring-bone" wise. When you enter the shop you will notice the great diagonal beam with the joists framed into it, crossing each other at right angles.

* "Surrey Archæological Collections," vol. iv.
† "The Charm of the English Village" (Batsford).

CHILDS WICKHAM, NEAR EVESHAM, WORCESTER.

LONG WITTENHAM, BERKS

THIS beautiful cross stands in the little Berkshire village Long Wittenham. It suffered from Puritan iconoclastic zeal and lost its head; but it has now been restored. It is situated in the centre of the village, surrounded by a small green with some picturesque thatched cottages having dormer windows nestling amidst the thatch. The village used to be known as Earl's Wittenham, and also as Wittenham Abbots, as it formerly belonged to the priory of Longueville Giffard, in the diocese of Rouen. Probably the monks reared this cross and built the first church; but as the monastery to which the village belonged was an alien priory, Henry V. deprived the monks of their property. Wittenham is a remarkable instance of the continuity of village life, as it is explained in the text.

This shop was built in the fifteenth century, and has performed its useful mission ever since. The most curious feature of these old shops is the arrangement of the wooden shutter that took the place of the window. It was closed at night, and, being fastened on hinges, was let down during the day and fastened at right angles to the wall, thus serving as a means for the display of the shopman's goods. Sometimes there were two shutters, and when they were opened the upper one formed a penthouse roof while the lower performed the duty already described. Loving care has guarded this old Lingfield shop during the several centuries of its usefulness. It has a glass window now instead of the discarded shutter. Glass windows were introduced into shop-windows in the eighteenth century; until that time the fronts of village shops were very similar to that at Lingfield, and did not offer any tempting bait to the attacks of the hammers of militant suffragettes.

In several of our illustrations the artist has depicted a village inn, which usually stands in the " street," a conspicuous and plea-sant-looking building. It is the village inn, and is known as the " Bull," or the " Bear," or the " Lion," or other beast or bird or other designation. The story of signboards alone is worthy of a volume, and country inns have a lore that would take long to tell. The signs are heraldic, and are often taken from the armorial bearings of some great family which owned the manor or held influence in the place. Our village inn at Barkham is called the " Bull," and

# THE COTTAGES AND VILLAGE

I doubt not that it was so named after the once distinguished family of Bullock, who held sway here as lords of the manor in the fifteenth and sixteenth centuries. We will examine the signs more closely presently, and note the curious examples of rustic humour which some of them suggest.

Inns can boast of great antiquity. Before the dissolution of monasteries poor travellers were often entertained at their guest-houses, while nobles and rich men were often the guests of the abbot. Rectors and vicars also recognised it as part of their duties to entertain strangers, and often had commodious stables for the accommodation of the horses of the guests. But even in the mediæval times there were inns, and some not very favourable pictures have been drawn of them by poets and satirists. Skelton, the tutor of Henry VIII., describes a tavern at Leatherhead near the high-road, and its not very prepossessing landlady:

> Her skynne lose and slacke,
> Grained like a sacke,
> With a crooked backe.
> She breweth noppy ale,
> And maketh thereof port sale
> To travellers, to tynkers,
> To sweters, to swynkers,
> And all good ale drinkers.

"Piers the Plowman's" description of an inn a century earlier is not more favourable, and the literature of inns tells of Chaucer's pilgrims refreshing themselves at a wayside hostelry.

After the Reformation and the disappearance of the monastic guest-house inns became more common, but it was not until the coaching days dawned that they began to flourish and thrive and attain to their highest pitch of prosperity and usefulness. As I have said in my book on "English Villages":* "The old village inn has its own story to tell of the old coaching days, and of the great people who used to travel along the main road, and were sometimes snowed up in a drift just below 'The Magpie,' which had always good accommodation for travellers and stabling for fifty horses. All was activity in the stable-yard when the coach came in; the villagers crowded round the inn doors to see the great folks from London who were regaling themselves with well-cooked English joints; and if they stayed all night, could find comfortable beds with lavender-scented sheets, and every attention." Motors now speed along in the track of the old coaches, but their hideous hoot is less musical than the cheerful post-horn. When the coaches ceased to run and railways came in, the decline and fall of the old inn was rapid. It is now a simple ale-house, where the villagers foregather in the evenings and discuss the affairs of the nation and the more important doings of the countryside with the animation born of sundry mugs of ale. Nothing disturbs its placid existence, save the annual dinner of the cricket club or a beanfeast.

Sad was the fate of the old coachman. He was a great man in the days of his prime. We can see him in imagination descending

* Methuen and Co.

139

from his box and hear his usual time-honoured jokes. He was held in great awe by the village urchins, and in spite of his good-tempered, rubicund face, he was a terrible rascal. Like the old-fashioned sailor, he had a wife in every port. Old friends of mine tell me that when, as young boys, they were going to school on a coach the old Jehu would, by threats or persuasions, make them give up to him all the pocket-money they had in their possession. Retributive justice condemned him to the poor-house when coaches vanished and the shriek of the railway engine extinguished the sound of the post-horn. But in the days of his prime he was a very merry-looking personage, who cracked his whip, could take a fly off his leader's ear, and drive—well, no words can describe his wondrous skill. In slippery weather, when the nags could scarce keep to their feet, through drifts of snow, up hill, down dale, there was never a surer hand for the reins, never a braver heart or a character endowed with a more indomitable perseverance. Peace to his ashes!

The village inn was an important building even in hamlets through which no coaches ran. There the village club or benefit society held its sessions, and the rector gave an annual dinner to all the farmers who paid tithe to him. If the tithe amounted to only a few shillings the farmer was very careful to consume the whole amount in the food and drink that were provided. There was usually a bowling-green attached to the house, and thither came the squires and gentry of the neighbourhood, and sometimes their ladies also, to partake in a friendly game at this old-fashioned pastime. At the " Shoulder of Mutton " or the " Warren Arms " the hounds used to have, and still have, favourite meets, and the inn was alive with animation, huntsmen and hounds on the green before the door, maids running about full of excitement, bearing stirrup-cups to the riders, men leading horses up and down in front of the house, while the Master and the squires of the neighbourhood regaled themselves within until all were ready to start for the coverts to draw the fox. Hunting a hundred years ago commenced at a much earlier hour than at present. We usually meet at the comfortable hour of eleven o'clock. Horses are sent on to the meet and their owners drive up in a motor-car, discard their fur coats, mount their steeds, and are ready for a run. Formerly the riders would start from home at five or six o'clock, before daybreak, and ride a dozen miles to the meet. But they usually finished the day much earlier, and would never draw for a fresh fox after one o'clock. Sometimes they would stay at the inn for a hearty dinner and refreshment, smoking church-warden pipes and singing some of those quaint hunting songs and ballads which have come down to us and were often composed by one of the party who had a turn for verse. Perhaps I may be pardoned for mentioning an old hunting song which records the numerous misfortunes that befell a company of hunters on one unlucky day's hunting, when an ancestor of mine with one other squire were the only ones who escaped. I wish I knew the whole

Village Cross, Ashton-under-Hill, Gloucester.

Dickens also describes another comfortable roadside inn on the Marlborough Downs, where Tom Smart found comfort and refreshment and, incidentally, a wife, one stormy evening when the cheerful lights of its windows attracted the cold and weary traveller. It was a charming old house with a deep porch and gable-topped windows, and within the blazing fire burning in the grate invited the slippered feet of Tom Smart, no less than the neat chambermaid who laid the table for supper, and the rows of green bottles with gold labels, and jars of pickles and preserves, and cheeses and boiled hams, and rounds of beef and other delectable foods. No wonder Tom married the buxom owner of all these creature comforts. But the description is useful for our purpose in conveying to us modern folk the comforts and resources of an old-fashioned roadside inn of the early eighteenth century.

This reputation of good inns in England dates back to the beginning of the seventeenth century. Fynes Morrison wrote in 1617 of their comforts :

" The world affords not such inns as England hath, for as soon as the passenger comes the servants run to him ; one takes his horse and walks him till he be cold, then rubs him and gives him meat ; but let the master look to this point. Another gives the traveller his private chamber and kindles his fire, the third pulls off his boots and makes them clean ; then the host or hostess visits him—if he will eat with the host—or at a common table it will be 4d. and 6d. If a gentleman has his own chamber, his ways are consulted, and he has music, too, if he likes."

We need not stop to record the sayings of great men who have sung the praises of inns, of Dr. Johnson, Shenstone, Archbishop Leighton, and a score of others who have repeated the poet's sentiments :

> Whoe'er has travelled life's dull road,
>     Where'er his stages may have been,
> May sigh to think he still has found
>     The warmest welcome at an inn.

And therein the old-fashioned hostelry differs from its modern counterpart. In the new grand caravansera you receive no welcome. You have no individuality; you are only a number. You come, you go, and no one cares, unless the liberality of your "tips" surprises a supercilious and gorgeous porter into a transient show of interest, or contrives to extract a reluctant expression of gratitude from a hurrying German waiter. It was not so in olden days. Then you were an honoured guest, and all the resources of the country inn were taxed to make you comfortable. As this book is travelling to America I must not forget to record Washington Irving's opinion of our English inns, to whom they strongly appealed, and who, when describing his visit to the shrine of Shakespeare, thus wrote :

" To a homeless man, who has no spot on this wide world which he can truly call his own, there is a momentary feeling of something like independence and territorial consequence when, after a weary day's travel, he kicks off his boots, thrusts his feet into slippers, and stretches himself before an inn fire. Let the world without go as it may ; let kingdoms rise or fall, so long as he has the wherewithal to pay his bill, he is for the time being the very monarch of all he surveys. ' Shall I not take mine ease in mine inn ? ' thought I, as I gave the fire a stir, lolled back in my elbow-chair, and cast a complacent look about the little parlour of the Red House at Stratford-on-Avon."

In another passage, too long to quote, he tells further of his appreciation of the homely village inn.

Looking up at the sign-board before entering, we notice that our inn bears the sign of the "Five Alls," a not uncommon inn name in the West Country. We were curious to know what it signified ; and that is not an uncommon feeling when you try to discover the mysteries of signs. Our curiosity was satisfied by our host, who informed us that these "Five Alls" are meant to signify

> I rule all (the King).
> I pray for all (the Bishop).
> I plead for all (the Barrister).
> I fight for all (the soldier).
> I pay for all (the farmer).

The oldest inn sign is a bush hung above the door. The old proverb "Good wine needs no bush" records its popularity, and the mediæval poet sings of

# THE COTTAGES AND VILLAGE

The greene busche that hangeth out
Is a sygne . . .
That within is wyne to selle.

In our country villages we prefer signs that relate to country pursuits, such as the " Plough," the " Wheatsheaf," the " Barley-corn," and when the clothiers and wool-merchants plied their trade, and the rustics spun wool, and every week the merchants sent out their pack-horses and collectors to bring in the results of the rural industry, such signs as the " Woolpack," the " Fleece " and the " Pack-horse " came into fashion.

When the village was owned by some important family its arms or cognisance would supply a sign for the village inn. Thus the " Lion " depicted in various colours adorns many a signboard, or the " White Hart," or the " Blue Boar." At Grantham every animal is blue, and we see a Blue Horse, a Blue Ram, a Blue Sheep, and many other cerulean animals and objects, proclaiming the political colour of the great neighbouring landowner. The " Eagle and Child " is the crest of the Stanley family and the Earls of Derby. Hence it is a favourite sign in Lancashire, where it is popularly known among the rustics as " Brid and Babby," the vernacular for Bird and Baby. There is an interesting legend with regard to the origin of the cognisance, but it would take too long a space to tell it here, and I have recorded it elsewhere.*

* " Legends of Lancashire," in " Memorials of Old Lancashire " (Messrs. G. Allen and Sons).

146

And then we find that the sports and games of the countryside are reflected on the signboards. What more constant sign do we find than the " Bat and Ball," or the " Cricketers' Arms " ? It carries our thoughts back to the old village cricket matches, such

INN KITCHEN, KENT

as Miss Mitford loved to describe, when the pitch was not as level as a billiard-board, when all the bowling was under-hand, and the " swells " in the team wore tall hats, and there was much rivalry between Tom the Blacksmith and Master Brown, the sporting young farmer, for the hand of sweet Peggy Trueman, and each swain, like gallant knights of old, strove to distinguish himself before the lady's eyes, in order to win her favour and gain her love.

147

# THE COTTAGES AND VILLAGE

The "Cock," the "Fighting Cock," and the "Bantam Cock" tell of the old sport of cock-fighting, which, happily, with bull-baiting and other cruel sports, has long since passed away.

Villagers are not lacking in wit, but their humour is curious. Your jokes would scarcely raise a smile on their homely faces, and perhaps theirs would scarcely amuse you. Thus when you see the sign of the "Three Loggerheads," and you discover only two figures of stupid-looking rustics, and you ask wonderingly why the artist has not painted a third, you discover that you yourself are the victim of this rural pleasantry. It is a wonder that militant suffragettes should not have waged war with hammers on the "Silent Woman." It stands as an insult to the ladies, as it basely implies that the only way to make a woman silent is to cut off her head. The "Load of Mischief" is an equal reflection on the fair sex, representing a man staggering under the weight of a woman, who is on his back. She is holding a glass of gin in her hand ; a chain and padlock are round the man's neck, labelled "Wedlock." On the right-hand side is the shop of "S. Gripe, Pawnbroker," and a carpenter is just going to pledge his tools. Hogarth was the painter of the original sign, which appears not only in the town of Wallingford and the city of Norwich, but in country villages such as Blewbury, in Berkshire.

Rustic humour, conscious or unconscious, has converted many old signs into something quite different. Thus they have transformed the "Elephant and Castle" into "Pig and Tinder Box."

Possibly the artist's delineation of an elephant was not very realistic, and resembled more a pig than the more massive quadruped. The "Bacchanals" they converted into "Bag-o'-Nails," and the Puritan "God encompasses us" into "Goat and

KENTISH INN KITCHEN

Compasses." There are many other examples of these strange transformations, and as they are well known they need not here be enumerated.

But the glory of the old inns has departed. No longer does the coach drive up to its door and disgorge its fashionable and interesting passengers. It is but an ale-house now, where the rustics congregate in the evening, and even they look somewhat ashamed when they are seen to enter. But in the old village life of the place the inn has played a prominent part. It is still a picturesque object, and retains evidences of its former greatness. And as travellers wearied with our long tramp we rest awhile in its old-world garden, drink our cups of tea beneath the shade of the orchard trees, see the old bowling-green where knights and squires used to contend in days gone by in the presence of their dames and guests, amongst whom we recognise a Court beauty of the time of the Merry Monarch, we reflect upon this striking feature of old village life, and, like Falstaff, " take our ease at an inn."

# XIV

## VILLAGE REVELRY

LIFE in our village passes placidly along, like the course of a deep, gently flowing river. Its tranquil existence is not perturbed by sudden wild alarms. Not even the arrival of newspapers or the prevalence of industrial strife in other less-favoured shires of England can disturb our peace. It was so in former days. It is still the same. Read the diaries of the Squires of Hickstead Place, in Sussex, written in the seventeenth century. They cover the years from 1657 to 1738, a very interesting and important period in English history. And yet life passed so quietly and uneventfully in the little Sussex homestead that nothing is recorded of the great events that were happening in England. The death of Oliver Cromwell, the restoration of the monarchy, the rule of the second Charles, the plots and conspiracies, the rebellion of Monmouth, the accession of James II., his flight and the revolution, the Jacobite risings—all these were of no account to the Stapleys, the Squires of Hickstead. They spent their lives in tending their cattle, looking after their farms and their families, and troubled themselves no more about the political events of far-reaching importance than if these had occurred in another country or another planet. It is true we have railways near us now, and we sometimes travel by them, and hear the great news of the world; but still the village life flows on quite evenly, undisturbed by the world's rude noise.

But is it not all very dull? asks the town-bred person. We do not find it so. We are a little more restless than of yore, and sometimes our villagers are tempted to forsake our green meadows and cottage homes and to migrate to towns. But they generally wish to return, and discover, too late, that the streets of London are not paved with gold, and that they were better off in the country.

It is true that country life is not so gay as it was in former days; and the labourer no longer takes delight in the simple pleasures that delighted his forefathers. He is slow of foot and has forgotten how to take his part in rustic revels, or to dance the old country dances for which England was famous. Even their names are almost forgotten, and can only with difficulty be recovered from the old folks when they can be induced to talk of the days when they could dance "The Maid of the Mill," and "Bob Joan," "The Green Garters," and "Constant Billy." These dances were not really country dances at all, but *contre-dances*,* the partners standing opposite to each other, the men forming one line, the

* I have described these dances at length in my book on "Old English Customs" (Methuen & Co.), and the words and tunes were kindly taken down for me by a friend who discovered them at Bampton, in Oxfordshire.

COTTAGE DOOR, ELMLEY CASTLE, WORCESTER.

FOOTBRIDGE, NEAR PORLOCK, SOMERSET.

women another, as in " Sir Roger de Coverley," sole relic of these ancient modes. They all sang, too, as they danced, such blithe verses as

> There were fifty fair maidens that
>  Sport on the green,
> I gazed on them well as you see,
> But the maid of the mill,
>  The maid of the mill,
> The maid of the mill for me.
> She is straight and tall as a poplar-tree,
>  Her cheeks are red as a rose ;
> She is one of the fairest young girls I see,
>  When dress'd in her Sunday clothes.

One day in the year was a " red-letter day." It was the village Revel, which Mr. Baring-Gould has so pleasantly described in one of his novels. He says that sixty years ago it was a gladsome festival, to which all the youths and maids looked forward for half the year and looked back on through the other half. It was the great event in the year's history which formed the general subject of conversation. It has nearly vanished now in most villages. There were horse-races, wrestling matches and merry-go-rounds, and peep-shows and menageries and waxworks, and booths and stalls for the sale of gingerbread and ribbons and laces, toys and brooches, and cocoanut "shies" and "all the fun of the fair." The cheapjack, too, came with his waggon and made every one roar with laughter at his merry jokes and quaint buffoonery. Gipsies pitched their tents on the green, and the men rode in the races

# THE COTTAGES AND VILLAGE

bonfires on Guy Fawkes Day. All these brought life and animation to the village and redeemed rural life from its dulness and prevented monotony. And besides these various diversions, which were common throughout England, many districts and

REMAINS OF QUINTAIN, AT OFFHAM, KENT

villages had their own peculiar customs which marked their individuality and dated back to a remote past. It is a pity that these should be allowed to die and thus to sever our connection with the past life of the village and to diminish the heritage of customs bequeathed to us by our ancestors.

In the little village of Offham, in Kent, there is an interesting relic of ancient pastimes. It is a quintain, a memorial of the days of chivalry, when knights tilted at tournaments and won the applause of Queens of Beauty in the lists. There were various forms of quintains, which afforded good practice in tilting. We cannot describe all these forms.* That at Offham is one of the simpler kinds, consisting of a post with a cross-piece that turns on a pivot. At one end was placed a shield, at the other a bag of sand. The rider rode with his lance in rest to attack the shield. If he missed it he incurred the scorn of the spectators ; but if he struck it and rode not fast, the cross-piece would swing round and he would receive a sound blow upon his neck from the bag of sand. It is well that this interesting relic of ancient sport should have been preserved.

In many of the sketches of villages and cottages that appear in this book our artist has not forgotten to depict children, who are the life and soul of the village. We elders may have grown too old and too wise to delight in the simple games and diversions that pleased our more simple-minded sires. But the children do not forget their games, and I have often wondered what is the origin of those unwritten laws that govern the yearly course of their various pastimes. Now the youngsters are trundling their hoops as they merrily run to and fro from school. In a short time marbles will be the rage ; then that dangerous game called " piggy," or tip-cat. Now the girls will be skipping, soon they will be marking the roads with mysterious lines and playing " hop-scotch." Then tops will be fashionable, and so on, through the year. Can

* *Cf.* Strutt's "Sports and Pastimes."

157

no one account for this curious and invariable order, which no self-respecting boy or girl can dare to transgress? " Look at 'im now, playing tip-cat in the marble season," scornfully says a jealous suitor, aged nine, pointing to his rival. An order of the Medes and Persians is nothing to that which governs children's games. Moreover, it is, I believe, universal in its application; it is not confined to particular districts. Whence is it derived? Who first framed this unwritten law?

There is a mystery, too, about the girls' singing games. Whence did they acquire those curious words and tunes which they sing so blithely as they join hands and dance round in a circle? The singing tunes are quaint and traditional, pretty and haunting. Both tunes and rhymes vary in different parts of England. Berkshire children have some very charming verses, and no one can tell who invented them. Very pleasant is the melody of

Isabella, Isabella, Isabella, farewell.
Last night when I parted
I left her broken-hearted.
Beside the green bushes there stands a young man.
Choose your lover [*repeated twice*]—farewell.
Open the gates, love [*repeated twice*]—farewell.
Go to church, love [*repeated twice*]—farewell.
Kneel down, love [*repeated twice*]—farewell.
Say your prayers, love [*repeated twice*]—farewell.
Put on the ring, love [*repeated twice*]—farewell.
Stand up, love [*repeated twice*]—farewell.
In the ring, love [*repeated twice*]—farewell.
Kiss together, love [*repeated twice*]—farewell.

ALLERFORD, SOMERSET.

WEST HAGBOURNE, BERKS

WEST HAGBOURNE cannot compare with its sister village, East Hagbourne, with regard to the beauty of its buildings. Without being anything remarkable, " it is just one of those tranquil villages making the true country of England the home of placid pleasure," as some one has written of its charm. The sketch shows a peaceful rural scene with two cottages roofed with weather-beaten thatch, probably built at the end of the seventeenth century, one of two storeys, and the other of one, with attics under the roof. They are of half-timber construction, the spaces between the upright and horizontal timber being filled with brick or wattle, and covered with plaster. Giant sunflowers adorn the garden.

"Nuts in May" is common to many counties, and is altogether delightful. The girls arrange themselves in two lines. One line advances, singing :

> Here we come gathering nuts in May,
> Nuts in May, nuts in May ;
> Here we come gathering nuts in May,
> This cold and frosty morning.

There are sixteen other lines which we have not space to quote. A champion is chosen from one side who meets the representative of the other side, and then ensues a tug-of-war, and the captive one joins the line of the conqueror. And so the game goes on until one side gathers all the " nuts."

And then we have " Jenny Jones," which has a Welsh sound, and there is also an entirely Welsh version of this pathetic little ballad. One of the children kneels down behind her guardian. The rest advance and say, " We've come to see Jenny Jones " ; but the guardian tells them that she is busy washing, or ironing, or starching ; and then that she is ill, dying, and at last dead And then they ask what colour they should wear—red, or blue, or white ; but the only suitable attire is black, as poor Jenny has to be buried. So they seize poor Jenny and carry her away, marching in a sad procession behind the " corpse " with aprons to their eyes.

Such are some of their games, and there are many others, such as " The Three Lodgers," " Oranges and Lemons," " The Three Dukes," " Old Roger."

# THE COTTAGES AND VILLAGE

The following must be a very ancient rhyme, as centuries ago the last wolf in England died:

> Sheep, sheep, come home.
> > Afraid !
> What are you afraid of ?
> > Wolf !
> Wolf is gone to Devonshire,
> And will not be back for seven year,
> > So sheep, sheep, come home.

" The Old Woman from Cumberland," " Rosy Apple," " Winny winny wee," " The Lady on the Mountain," " Queen Anne," " The Leaves are Green," are some of the singing games which delight our rustic maidens, and puzzle us as to their origin and meaning.

But in spite of the song of the children village life is not so gay and bright as it used to be, though wages are higher and the wolf of poverty is no longer prowling about the doors of our cottages. His howl has often been heard, creating terror and alarm in the hearts of its hearers, and restraining the sounds of joy and rural revelry. When the price of food was high and wages were low, and there was not enough bread to feed the children, whose pinched faces cried silently for food, there was little chance of happiness. It was so in the " hungry forties " ; it was so at the end of the eighteenth and in the beginning of the nineteenth centuries. And one of the most authoritative writers on the social history of that period was the Reverend David Davies, my most worthy predecessor at Barkham, who occupied this study chair (or rather its forerunner) and with most careful investigation and laborious research wrote a work entitled " The Case of Labourers in Husbandry" (1795). That was a period of growing discontent. The rich complained loudly of the great and rapid increase in the poor rate, and the poor bitterly of the little benefit they derived from it. Dr. Davies attributed this sad state of affairs to the increased prices of food, and set himself the task of determining the condition of the rural poor at different periods in the fourteenth, fifteenth, sixteenth, and seventeenth centuries. He discovered much that was disastrous, and his book made a profound impression on contemporary observers. Howlett called it "incomparable," and the author of a recent book on " The Village Labourer" states that it is impossible for the modern reader to resist its atmosphere of reality and truth. " This country parson gives us a simple, faithful, and sincere picture of the facts, seen without illusion or prejudice, and free from all the conventional affectations of the time : a priceless legacy to those who are impatient of the generalisations with which the rich dismiss the poor."

The General Enclosure Act of 1845, the results of which were aptly described in the rhyme,

> A sin it is in man or woman
> To steal a goose from off a common ;
> But he doth sin without excuse
> Who steals the common from the goose,

had not, of course, then been passed.

# THE COTTAGES AND VILLAGE

The old Rector of Barkham strongly advised that in every enclosure a certain quantity of land should be reserved for cottagers and labourers. " Allow to the cottager," he wrote, " a little land about his dwelling for keeping a cow, for planting potatoes, for raising flax or hemp. Convert the waste lands of the kingdom into small arable farms, a certain quantity every year to be let on favourable terms to industrious families ; and restrain the engrossment and over-enlargement of farms. The propriety of these measures cannot, I think, be questioned."

If the voice of my revered predecessor had been listened to, it would have saved the necessity of passing " Small Holdings Acts," and rendered the condition of our labourers far more agreeable. He is far less famous than he deserves to be. It is true that his name appears in the " Dictionary of National Biography," with a few details of his life ; but the world knows nothing of him. He was methodical in the extreme, as the careful way in which he kept our register books discloses, and I have his private account-book, which tells much of his life's story. I hope to reveal its contents some day, but we have no space for that in this present work.

In listening to the sounds of rural revelry we must not forget to hear the howls of the dreaded wolf that sometimes came prowling around our doors. He may perchance come again when we least expect him. Happy will he be who will slay the monster, and ever keep our homes free from its approach.

# LIFE OF RURAL ENGLAND

In some villages rural life has completely changed during the last twenty years. Some have degenerated into being but a suburb of a fashionable colony of villas. The rustic's old semi-independent life—haymaking, thatching, harvesting, turf-cutting, hop-picking—is all gone. He took a pride and interest in his work and in his village. But the farms are all broken up, and villas cover the fields and sometimes have supplanted the cottages, and the rustic who remains tends the strips of villa gardens or drives a coal cart and his wife goes out charing. The old village life has died out and gone for ever.

But such villages are comparatively few, and our illustrations show many unspoilt hamlets where the life goes on uninterruptedly and pleasantly ; and if we are not so boisterous as our forefathers in our mirth and revelry, there is still much quiet enjoyment. Country life is wonderfully attractive to those who love Nature. It has its hardships, as all lives have, but we, whose lot it is to live among the green fields of rural England, agree with Roscoe when he said : " If I were asked who I considered the happiest of the human race, I would answer, those who cultivate the earth with their own hands."

# XV

## VILLAGE INDUSTRIES

IN olden days before railways were invented, when roads were often impassable and communication between towns difficult, every village was a self-centred community and provided for its own needs. The people did not travel to London or the nearest town when they wanted a new coat or their shoes to be mended, or a new scythe, or to be shaved. In every village there were tradesfolk, artisans and labourers for the providing of every sort of requirement which the inhabitants might need. Take, for example, the little village of Soulbury, in the county of Buckingham. It is quite a small place of about two hundred inhabitants, and yet it could supply all its own needs. The parish registers disclose this. The vicars at the end of the seventeenth and the beginning of the eighteenth century were kind enough to record the trade or profession of those whose names they had occasion to indite in the register books; and being scholars they preferred to record them in Latin. Thus we find a *molendarius*, or miller; several *firmarii* or *agricolæ*, or farmers; a *lactarius*, or milkman; a *rotarius*, or wheelwright; a *faber ferriaris*, or blacksmith or iron-worker; a *scissor*, or tailor; yeomen who farmed their own land; a *faber lignaris*, or carpenter; a *pistor*, or pounder or baker; a *hortulans*, or gardener; a *lanius*, or butcher; a *textor*, or weaver; a *brasiat*, or brazier; a grocer (the good vicar could not find a convenient Latin equivalent for this tradesman); a *cæmentarius*, or quarryman; a *sutor*, or cobbler or shoemaker; dairyman; a *lapicida*, or stone-cutter. And besides these there are the following occupations recorded in English, a little later: cordwainer or shoemaker, cooper, bricklayer, sack-carrier, chairman, publican, woodmonger, and pump-maker. In addition there were also the *generosi*, or men of good family, and labourers— a fairly good list of representative trades for a small country place. Other villages could furnish even larger returns, and show how capable they were in supplying all that was necessary for the carrying on of the life and work of the community.

Our artist has discovered a fair and beautiful water-mill at Elmley Castle, in Worcestershire, which tells of one of England's most ancient industries. It wears the marks and wrinkles of time, which only serve to enhance its beauties. Its aged beams and timbers have had to be supported by props. The thatch of the roof is seamed and scarred and ruffled by the storms of many winters. But nothing can destroy its beauty, whether seen with our own eyes or depicted by the skilled brush of the artist.

Time was when our villages in Berkshire and the Cotswolds, and in other parts of England, were busy hives of industry in the days when the cloth trade flourished. The writer of " The

# THE COTTAGES AND VILLAGE

Pleasant History of Thomas of Reading or the Sixe Worthie Yeomen of the West " wrote that " Among all crafts this was the only chief, for that it was the greatest merchandise, by the which our country became famous throughout all nations. And it was wisely thought that the one-half of the people in the land lived in those days thereby, and in such good sort, that in the common-wealth there were few or no beggars at all; poor people whom God had blessed with most children did by means of this occupation so order them that when they were come to five or seven years of age they were able to get their own bread. Therefore it was not without cause that clothiers were both honoured and loved."

This cloth trade gave employment to the people in the villages as well as in the towns, where there were spinners and carders and sheremen and fullers and dyers and shuttle-makers and tearers and weavers and a host of others. Before the dissolution of the monasteries the sleepy old towns of the Cotswolds were prosperous clothing centres. In the churches there are memorials of worthy merchants and woolmen; and evidences of the bounty of the clothiers are seen in restored and rebuilt churches, in charities and almshouses. As one of them piously exclaimed,

I thank God, and ever shall ;
It was the sheep that paid for all.

In old towns such as Coventry, and large villages, you can still see the long rows of windows on the second floor of the houses,

The Bell Inn, Waltham St. Laurence, Berkshire.

MONKS ELEIGH, SUFFOLK.

so built in order to give light to the weavers as they worked at their looms. They remain still at the old-world village of Kersey, which gave its name to a kind of cloth woven there, and of which our artist gives a drawing. In the beautiful Stroud Valley the cloth trade lingers on, but it was a sad day for our southern clothiers when steam was invented, for steam-power requires coal, and coal can only be procured in certain districts, and the northern clothiers were crafty men who found out many inventions, spinning-jennies, carding-machines, and suchlike things; hence the tide of fortune turned elsewhere, and the hand-loom is as dead as Queen Anne. In the days of my youth I well remember seeing hand-looms in cottages, but these were used for weaving silk, about which much could be said if we had space. The trade does not seem to have been much practised in England before 1585. James I. was very eager to promote it, and silk-weaving and the knitting of silk stockings were carried on in many small towns and villages, the women and children knitting the stockings at home and bringing them to their employer. Near where I am writing in many of the old gardens there are mulberry-trees which were planted for the feeding of silkworms.

Towcester, in Northamptonshire, was also famous for its silk stockings, and near it is Abthorpe, which has an inn called " The Stocking Frame," a relic of its ancient industry.

Special industries cling to certain places and localities. I have recorded several of these in my book on " The Charm of English

Villages,'' and may not repeat them. But I have not recorded the diversity of our cheeses. Certain cheeses belong to special places, such as Cheddar cheese, which only comes from the charming Somerset village where the caves are, or Cheshire, or Stilton, which, however, is not made at the place so named, but was sold there at the famous Bell Inn, where the coaches stopped on their way to York, and thus acquired the name of Stilton. The best of all, as far as my judgment goes, comes from the Yorkshire Wensleydale, which may not be despised.

Buckinghamshire villagers still make beautiful lace, owing to the encouragement they receive from the North Bucks Lace Association. The art came to the county with certain Flemish refugees who fled to England about 1570, and settled at Olney, Newport Pagnell, and other neighbouring villages. In the seventeenth century the lace industry was most flourishing, and Bucks was the great lace-making centre of England. You have seen the lace-maker at work, doubtless, with her pillow on a stool in front of her, her design in horn parchment laid flat on it, and her bobbins and pins, some with sealing-wax heads, and her deft fingers rapidly moving the bobbins and weaving beautiful patterns that delight the eyes of the connoisseur. Cowper, who knew the lace-maker well, thus painted her picture in 1780 :

> Yon cottager, who weaves at her own door
> Pillow and bobbins, all her little store ;
> Content, though mean, and cheerful, if not gay,

Shuffling her threads about the livelong day,
Just earns a scanty pittance : and at night
Lies down secure, her heart and pocket light ;
She for her humble sphere by nature fit,
Has little understanding, and no wit ;
Receives no praise ; but though her lot be such
(Toilsome and indigent) she renders much ;
Just knows and knows no more, her Bible true—
A truth the brilliant Frenchman never knew ;
And in that charter reads with sparkling eyes
Her title to a treasure in the skies.

The lace-makers were very busy when gentlemen loved to adorn themselves with this material. King William the Third's bill for lace in one year amounted to £2459 19s., and he used it for handkerchiefs, cravats, razor-cloths, and night-shirts, and his Queen Mary spent £1918 a year on lace. Catherine of Aragon and her maids are said to have taught the Bucks folk the art, and a lace named after her is still made at Towcester. Newport Pagnell used to be the great central market for the trade, whence patterns were sent out to Olney, Hanslope, and elsewhere, and at the beginning of the last century the villagers of Hanslope used to make about £10,000 a year profit.

The " dentille d'Angleterre " was famous in Europe, so much so that in the seventeenth century the French makers used to appropriate that name for the product of their own manufacture. What is meant by bone lace ? The origin of the title is that the old lace-makers used sheep's trotters for bobbins, and as pins were an expensive item the bones of fish and birds were employed in lieu thereof. The machine-made lace of Nottingham caused the decline of this beautiful art; but if every fair lady would insist on bedecking herself with the genuine article we might hope to see our cottage women " a-sitting at their pillows, the bobbins plying merrily," as in the days of yore.

Particular villages sometimes have their own industries. Luton, in Bedfordshire, is famous for its straw-plaiting, which has a curious history. Mary Queen of Scots introduced the industry to Scotland from France, and King James I. transplanted it to England. He entrusted the care and protection of it to the family of the Napiers, who had their seat at Luton Hoo, the fine mansion situated a short distance from the village of Luton, formerly the home of Sir Thomas Boleyn, Anne Boleyn's father. So the Napiers taught the village folk the mystery of straw-plaiting, which still survives.

Northamptonshire is declared in an old proverb to be the least wooded but the most woaded of any county, referring to the old industry of cultivating woad for the dyers. A century ago there were still woad or "wad" grounds near Hardingstone, and "huts which the woaders lived in during the summer, while the work went on of growing the crop, cutting the leaves, and grinding them into a paste, which was made into balls and dried by the wind." *

* "Memorials of Old Northamptonshire," by Miss Dryden, p. 12.

THE MILL WHEEL, ELMLEY CASTLE, WORCESTER.

Houses formerly occupied by weavers, Kersey, Suffolk.

Barcherston, in Warwickshire, could once boast of a famous tapestry manufacture, which was established by one William Sheldon, a gentleman of Weston and Brailes and Beoley, described by Dugdale as one who *primus in Angliam suo sumptu tapeta texendi artum advexit*. He lived in the reign of Henry VIII., and sent one Richard Hyckes to the Netherlands to acquire the secrets of the art of tapestry-weaving. Looms were established at Barcheston, and produced some remarkable work, notably the wondrous maps of the counties of England which are still in existence in the Bodleian Library and the Museum at York. The industry continued until the beginning of the seventeenth century.

Witney and Woodstock produce gloves, and so also does the county of Worcester. The glovers of Worcester were incorporated in the reign of Henry VII., who granted them a charter, and much of the work was carried on in the neighbouring villages. Silent are the hammers of the ironworkers of Sussex. They were busy enough in former days, and the furnaces consumed much of the timber of the forest ridge of the county, "the fair daughters of the Weald," who,

> Foreseeing their decay each hour so fast come on,
> Under the axe's stroke, fetched many a grievous moan.

Of town-bred trades we take no account in this book, and we need not wander far through any countryside without finding some traces of rural industries. Alas! too often they have been allowed to die out, and changed economic conditions have transferred them elsewhere. It would be a happy thing for rural England if every cottage had its spinning-wheel, which now slumbers in some obscure attic or appears as an ornament in the squire's drawing-room, and if each hamlet had its trade. Free Trade is doubtless a blessing to the country, but we pay dearly for it in the loss of the many occupations and industries which once flourished in our villages, and are now decayed or dead.

# XVI

## L'ENVOYE

OUR tour of inspection of English cottages and of the village life of rural England is nearly finished. We have seen much that has interested us, many beautiful homes which the brush of the artist has brought vividly to our remembrance. Labour Members in the House of Commons, who are for the most part town-bred men and know little of rural England, and Radicals who wish to win the agricultural labourer's vote, sometimes speak disdainfully of the cottage homes of England, and call them huts and hovels ; but they know little of the affection with which the rustic regards his cottage. His garden is to him a paradise. He loves the old beams and rafters of his roof. An old labourer was compelled to leave his cottage for a time while his landlord was " doing it up." He was asked when he hoped to return to it, and when the workmen would have finished the work of restoration. "Haply, in a few weeks now ; but," he added, with a sad shake of his head, "it won't be like going home." The renovated house with all its added comforts and conveniences did not compensate him for its old-fashioned homeliness. My old parish clerk brought up a large family of children who are respectable members of society, in a cottage with only two rooms and one or two "outshots" of quite small dimensions. They had a great affection for their home, in spite of its smallness and quaintness ; and when, owing to the neglect and carelessness of an agent, the massive old chimney fell down and ruined the cottage, their consternation and sorrow were great. The old man used to spend his days in contemplating the ruined home, which so oppressed his spirits that he committed suicide in an outhouse in his orchard. That is a tragedy that I shall never forget. The office which he held carries our thoughts back to many old features of rural life —the Christmas carols that he and his companions used to sing with traditional words and tunes, which have suffered several transmutations in their course through the ages ; the old village orchestra which he used to lead, and the barrel organ in the church he used to play. He was an important official in our little village community who could ill be spared, but we have not presumed to appoint a successor. His affection for his old home is touching and affecting, and it is shared by most cottagers who live on an estate, and are not moved on each October to make room for others who possess not the virtues and merits of our older friends.

The future of the homes which we have described is not very assured, and possibly many of them will ere long disappear. The increased land taxes have borne heavily on the squires of England, many of whom have been compelled to sell their estates. The building and repair of cottages was always considered an act of charity, as such property is never remunerative. Some are let rent-free ; for others a trifling sum is required : but a landlord knows well that if he spends money on cottage-building he will scarcely ever obtain 2 per cent. on his outlay. With resources crippled by undue taxation, he is unable to expend money on the buildings on his estate ; and if he sells it there is no one to perform this duty. Hence old cottages fall into disrepair and few new ones are built. During the last three years 1689 cottages have been condemned and compulsorily closed, which might have been saved with a little judicious expenditure of money and converted into sanitary and sound dwellings. The housing question is a serious one in country districts, and we sigh in vain for some benevolent scheme, some real and efficient Housing Act which will preserve the old and provide new dwellings that are not an eyesore to the countryside.

Some cottages rank with more important houses, and have become historically famous. Great men—poets, heroes of the sword and the pen, painters, bishops—have sprung from cottage homes, and made them places of pilgrimage for lovers of history. There is Shakespeare's birthplace at Stratford-on-Avon, the little house with small rooms, its tiny irregular staircase, its collection of relics, its garden stocked with the poet's flowers. It is so well known both by Englishmen and Americans that it needs no description. Not far away is Mary Arden's cottage at Wilmcote, the home of Shakespeare's mother, an old red-tiled and gabled farmhouse, and Anne Hathaway's home, a quaintly thatched, irregular, half-timbered house, somewhat spoilt by the proximity of an ugly row of modern cottages, its garden abloom with old-fashioned flowers, worthy of the home of the poet's bride. No

ANNE HATHAWAY'S COTTAGE, SHOTTERY

portrait tells us of her beauty, but we may conclude that she was fair and winsome, as an old writer testifies, "To steal men's hearts Anne hath a way."

Milton's home at Chalfont St. Giles, in Buckinghamshire, is but a cottage, "a pretty box," as he described it, but it is redolent with the memories of the great poet, who finished there his immortal "Paradise Lost" and conceived "Paradise Regained" at the suggestion of his friend the Quaker Thomas Ellwood, as they sat together on a bench in the little garden while the birds sang their grand songs and the country flowers shed their sweet scent around. Some American admirers would fain have transported this sweet dwelling, gabled, oak-timbered, and vine-clad, to the United States ; but we English folk cannot spare it yet.

Not far from where I am writing is the home of Miss Mitford, the much-beloved authoress of " Our Village." The little hamlet which she has made immortal is Three Mile Cross, near Reading, in Berkshire, where the descendants live of those quaint people who appear in her book, and I often ride along a grassy lane near the tiny cottage where the authoress used to sit on the stump of a fallen tree and weave her romances and stories of village folk. She almost seems to be still there.

At the request of the Editor of the *Spectator*, a few months ago I wrote an article suggesting to the authorities of the National Trust that ere all English villages are spoilt by the pulling down of old farms and cottages and the erection of hideous buildings devised by the jerry-builder or the genius of an estate agent, they should purchase an ideal hamlet and preserve it as a memorial for future generations. The National Trust, like an angel of mercy, has descended upon many doomed houses, stayed the progress of decay, and secured their tenure for future ages. It has rescued many spots of sylvan beauty from the spoiler's hand. Could it not do the like for an English village ? Just now there is an opportunity for this benevolent work, as many estates are being sold, and an ideal village could easily be found for the National Trust to exercise its care upon. No sentimental reason prompts this scheme, no desire to preserve picturesque objects merely because they are pretty, or to protect old buildings merely because they are old. We wish to preserve the traditional style of good building as far as it can be rescued after the lapse of good taste which the last century witnessed. The preservation of a single homestead here and there will scarcely answer the purpose we have in view. It is the whole grouping of houses of various dates, size, and construction, the church and manor-house blending with the cottages of the poor, the inn and almshouse, the shop and farm, barn and dovecote, that reveal the unrivalled charm of the English village and proclaim the story of the social life of the past. All this is worth preserving ere the wave of destruction that is surging over rural England renders such a task impossible.

Perhaps our book, which reveals so many fair examples of the beauties of old England, may plead effectually for the preservation of an ideal village. It is well that old cottages and hamlets that our forefathers reared should be sketched, painted, photographed, and described. But it would be far better to keep intact the actual buildings, which if once destroyed can never be replaced.

And as we roam through England we find many such cottage associations. We love to call back the old village life, to hear the quaint talk of the people, to enter into their joys and sorrows, to understand their ways and thoughts. In spite of the noisy talk of the agitators and Socialists who seek to disturb our peace, we love to keep in the old ways and follow in the footsteps of our sires, and know well the speciousness of modern Socialistic propaganda. And as for our villages, we are quite content with them. We like not the legislation that compels the squire to sell his

October Evening at Steventon, Berkshire.

# INDEX

181

# INDEX

# INDEX

# INDEX

# INDEX